Familie: Verwandtschaft, die den Unterschied macht

Family: Kinship that matters

Beihefte zur Ökumenischen Rundschau Nr. 92

Familie: Verwandtschaft, die den Unterschied macht

Family: Kinship that matters

Herausgegeben von Gerard den Hertog
und Jan Roskovec

EVANGELISCHE VERLAGSANSTALT
Leipzig

Bibliographische Information der Deutschen Nationalbibliothek
Die Deutsche Bibliothek verzeichnet diese Publikation in der Deutschen Nationalbibliographie; detaillierte bibliographische Daten sind im Internet über http://dnb.dnb.de abrufbar.

Printed in Germany · H 7569

Das Buch wurde auf alterungsbeständigem Papier gedruckt.

Cover: Kai-Michael Gustmann, Leipzig
Coverfoto: © Frog 974 – Fotolia.com
Satz: Wouter Beinema
Druck und Binden: Hubert & Co., Göttingen

ISBN 978-3-374-03094-1
www.eva-leipzig.de

Preface

From the 21st until the 24th April of 2010, a number of Central and Eastern European Theological Faculties held a conference in Apeldoorn, The Netherlands. The central theme of that conference was: ›Family: Kinship that matters‹. Unlike marriage and child-rearing, the family as the ›womb‹ of kinship in which a person grows to become a unique human being, were hardly being dealt with theologically.

The observation that one can speak of an ›emerging world family crisis‹ (Don Browning) decides the actuality of this theme. In current-day Europe the point of reference is the autonomous self, a self that leads a life in social networks. The family has lost many of its traditional functions, amongst which that of being a ›school of humanity‹.

A representative selection of the contributions on the Apeldoorn conference are published in this volume. The central theme, »the family«, is approached from several points of view. It is analyzed from the approaches of biblical theology and history, and is discussed in both systematical and practical theological ways.

The first contribution to this volume is the opening lecture of the conference, in which Gerard den Hertog demonstrates the urgency of the theme. A second article positing the theme is of the hand of Petruschka Schaafsma, who details the ethical presuppositions and implications of recent sociological research into the family.

The next three articles are located on the terrain of biblical studies, a terrain well-represented in the conference. In a certain sense, Elöd Hodossy-Takács ties into the sociological questions Schaafsma also discussed. He takes a look at the place and significance of families in

Ancient Israel, also taking society and economy into account, as well as religion.

Andrea Pethö-Udvardi's theme, »Jakobs struggle with himself in the light of his encounter with God«, lies in the field of biblical studies as well. She oversteps the bounds of theology too, venturing onto the terrain of depth psychology.

Zsolt Gereb treats a new-testamentical theme: What do »obedience and love« mean in Colossians 3:18–4:1? These verses are a part of one of the household tables that, in New Testament letters, constitute mirrors from which we perceive how families lived together in the young Church.

Henk van den Belt sets time a millennium and a half forward to the Dutch refugee congregation in sixteenth-century England. Using source materials, he reconstructs the way of life of those families and the way in which their reformed churches handled the family. His contribution is titled »Families in the Dutch Stranger Church as Examples of Early Modern Families«.

Maarten Kater sketches some systematic theological lines in his concentrated contribution titled »Extended Family as a familia Dei: A small Family Picture«.

Two contributions are dedicated to a theme current in both Eastern and Western Europe, be it not on the same terms: homosexuality. Ad de Bruijne questions whether the traditional position is in need of amendment. Rinse Reeling Brouwer shows how urgent his theme, »Homosexuality and family for church and theology«, is.

The last contribution to this volume deals with so-called contextual therapy. Contextual therapy, though propagated widely throughout Northern America and Western Europe, is of Eastern European extraction. The theory has been developed by the Hungarian psychiatrist Ivan Böszörményi-Nagy. His therapy does not approach humans in an isolated fashion, but as members of family context. The therapy reasons from the assumption that a harmonious life within one's own family has a large impact on one's mental wellbeing.

About a half of the contributions to the conference could not be included in this volume for varying reasons. Below, a list is given of the remaining lectures and workshops:

Prof. dr. Jutta Hausmann, Familienmotivik in den Psalmen

Prof. dr. Teus Hofman, Oikos in Luke. A biblical-theological reflection

Prof. dr. Jenö Kiss, Theologische und ethische Perspektiven in biblischen Familienerzählungen. Biblische Familienerzählungen – gelesen aus der Perspektive der kontextuellen Vorgehensweise

Dr. Gert van Klinken, Lecture Dynamics in the evolution of Calvinist family life: the example of the Ter Apel village 1880-1940

Drs. Danielle van de Koot, Religious legacies in urban childrearing practices. A qualitative research

Dr. Jan Roskovec, Family in the Christian Beginnings. What Did Really Matter to Jesus, Paul and John?

Dr. Béres Tamás, The extended family of mankind and the human dignity. Systematic theological approaches

Dr. Wim van Vlastuin, Marriage in the eschaton

Dr. Lieke Werkman, Hands On – Hands Off. Tensions (Moral and Otherwise) in Current Dutch Family Policy

Dr. Maarten Wisse, »Honor your father and your mother.« A Systematic-Theological Account of the Family on the Basis of the Decalogue

Place of conference: Theologische Universiteit Apeldoorn

Contents / Inhalt

Familie als Lebensform und Lebensschule der Humanität

Gerard den Hertog

In dieser Konferenz beschäftigen wir uns mit der Familie. Oder präziser: mit dem Geflecht in das wir als Menschen hineingeboren werden: »kinship« auf Englisch, »Verwandtschaft« auf Deutsch. Es geht hier um Begriffe, die im tagtäglichen Sprachgebrauch nicht klar umrissen sind. Wir sollten sie darum zuerst mal genauer zu definieren versuchen, damit wir auch wissen, worüber wir uns auf dieser Konferenz gemeinsam besinnen wollen.

Die Unklarheit, die diesen Worten in den verschiedenen Sprachen anhaftet, hat erstens zu tun mit deren Unterschied. Ich bitte um Entschuldigung bei unseren tschechischen, slowakischen, ungarischen, rumänischen und bulgarischen Teilnehmern, dass ich einfach keine Ahnung habe, wie es in ihrer Muttersprache um die Wörter und Begriffe für Familie und Verwandtschaft bestellt ist. Ich weiß nur einigermaßen Bescheid, wo es um die beiden Verhandlungssprachen dieser Konferenz geht: Deutsch und Englisch. In diesen Sprachen sind die Wörter »Familie« und »family« nicht deckungsgleich, und auch das Niederländische hat noch mal seine eigenen Nuancen.

Von mehr Bedeutung noch als die sprachlichen Unterschiede und Unklarheiten aber sind die Entwicklungen in unseren Gesellschaften. In seinem Aufsatz ›World Family Trends‹ in ›The Cambridge Companion to Christian Ethics‹ aus dem Jahr 2001 stellt D.S. Browning fest, es zeichne sich eine »emerging world family crisis«[1] ab. Er führt das nötige statistische Material auf, um diese Behauptung zu untermauern. Wenn er das ausarbeitet, beschränkt er sich aber auf die Sphäre von Ehe und Beziehungsbildung – und das ist eigentlich weitgehend üblich. Falls man schon die weiteren Verbände der Familie und der Verwandtschaft – Eltern, Großeltern, Onkel, Tanten, Kusinen usw. – berücksichtigt, geschieht das meistens nur in historischem Sinn. »Das war einmal. « In den letzten Jahren aber sind die prägende Kraft und deshalb auch aktuelle Relevanz uns mehr präsent geworden. Es gibt von daher Anlass, uns auf dieser Konferenz gezielt mit der Familie zu beschäftigen.

1 Es war einmal ... die Großfamilie

Vor etwa dreißig Jahren habe ich einen Vortrag eines Deutschen Familiensoziologen gehört, an den ich mich lebhaft erinnere. Ob der Vortrag je gedruckt wurde, weiß ich nicht. Ich habe nur mein Gedächtnis und erinnere mich nicht einmal mehr an seinen Namen.

Dieser Soziologe skizzierte das Bild einer Bauern-Großfamilie im Schwarzwald, etwa Ende des neunzehnten Jahrhunderts. Unter dem einen Dach eines großen Bauernhofes wohnten mehrere Familien. In seinem Beispiel der *pater familias* mit seiner Frau – so waren die Verhältnisse damals –, etwa sechzig Jahre alt, und zwei Söhne mit ihren Familien – eventuelle Töchter heirateten normalerweise Bauernsöhne und traten dann in eine andere Großfamilie ein. Der Bauernhof war Familienbesitz, schon seit mehreren Generationen. Die Verbindungslinien zwischen Vergangenheit und Zukunft waren klar, sichtbar und selbstverständlich.

Wie ging es zu in diesen Großfamilien? Es existierte damals und dort noch die vor-industrielle Gesellschaft, in der die Familie mehr oder weniger auch Arbeitsgemeinschaft war. Sicher, auf einem Bauernhof lebte und arbeitete man gemeinsam, wie auch heute noch bis zu einem gewissen Grad. Anders aber als heute lebten damals mehrere Familien mit Arbeitern eng zusammen. Im Beispiel des Soziologen wuchsen die Kinder der beiden Söhne also zusammen auf. Die Kinder besuchten nur die Primarschule – und das nicht einmal immer und bis zum Ende. Ein

[1] D.S. Browning, World Family Trends, in: Robin Gill (ed.), The Cambridge Companion to Christian Ethics, Cambridge (UK) / New York (USA) 2001, 243-260 (Zitat 243).

wesentlicher(er) Teil ihrer Bildung fand zuhause statt und war praxisorientiert. Der Vater war nicht der einzige Mann in der Nähe der Jungen, der ihnen vertraut war und von dem sie etwas lernen konnten. Die Mutter hatte auch nicht ganz alleine die Erziehung ihrer Töchter zu betreuen, sondern sie konnte sich Rat holen bei der Schwägerin oder der Schwiegermutter.

Dennoch – wenn ich es so darstelle, ist es noch zu modern, zu konstruiert, als hätte man sich das so ausgedacht. So war es aber nicht. Allein schon weil man unter einem Dach wohnte, nahm man so oder so Teil an der Erziehung der Kinder. Das bedeutete einerseits Entlastung: es gab ja mehrere Familienmitglieder, die die Kinder begleiteten und beobachteten und nicht absichtlich, sondern meistens eher unbewusst zu ihrer Erziehung beitrugen. Stillschweigend waren die Eltern in dem Sinne entlastet, dass die Kinder auch ihre eigenen – täglichen und also intensiven – Kontakt hatten mit den Großeltern, mit einem Onkel und einer Tante, die je auf ihre Weise sich zu ihnen verhielten. Wenn die Frauen sich aktiv an der Arbeit auf dem Bauernhof beteiligten, etwa bei der Ernte im Sommer, kümmerte die Schwiegermutter sich sowieso um die Enkelkinder.

Die Eltern mussten also nicht je in ihrer Weise unbedingt sozusagen ›alles‹ für die Kinder – und für einander! – bedeuten, es gab ja andere die an der Erziehung teilnahmen, etwa dadurch, dass sie die Mädchen stricken und sticken lehrten, zumal wenn die eigene Mutter das nicht gerne und gut machte. Zur Großfamilie gehörten auch noch die Knechte und die Mädchen, die im Haus wohnten und mitarbeiteten und oft auch einfach Spaß daran hatten, den jungen Buben etwas beizubringen. Der Druck auf die »Kernfamilie« mit zwei Kindern, in der die Ehepartner alle familialen ›Rollen‹ selber wahrnehmen müssen, war hier erheblich gelindert.

Nein, ich beabsichtige nicht Ihnen ein romantisches Idealbild vorzuführen. Diese Großfamilien hatten auch ihre Schattenseiten. Es gab da ausgesprochene und unausgesprochene Herrschaftsverhältnisse. Nicht wenige Schwiegertöchter werden darunter gelitten haben, nicht ihre eigene Familie so gestalten zu können, wie sie es gern nach eigenen Ansichten gemacht hätten. Es war auch für die Kinder nicht immer ein Vergnügen, mehrere Leute um sich herum zu haben, die ungefragt zu ihrer Erziehung beitrugen. Machen wir uns keine Illusionen.

Ich beabsichtige also nicht, eine ideale Vergangenheit zu zeichnen. Die früheren Zeiten kehren aber nicht wieder und so gut, wie manche sie gerne darstellen, waren sie auch nicht. Zudem gibt es auch Errungenschaften der letzten Dekaden, hinter die wir auch nicht zurückgehen möchten. Also: »Sprich nicht: Wie kommt's, dass die früheren Tage besser waren als diese? Denn du fragst das nicht in Weisheit. « (Pred 7,10) Es geht mir nur darum, uns ein bestimmtes Bild vor Augen zu führen, woher wir kommen – und zwar aus einer Vergangenheit, die kaum mehr als ein Jahrhundert her ist. Es kann und soll uns den Blick dafür schärfen, was alles sich geändert hat.

2 Individuelle Selbstbestimmung und Familie

Wenn wir diesem Bild der Großfamilie ein Zitat von Dorien Pessers, Professorin für Jura – Rechtstheorie – und auch aktiv (oder aktiv gewesen) als Dozentin für Frauenstudien, zur Seite stellen, zeigt sich gleich, was sich geändert hat:

> »Unter Einfluss einer in politischer Hinsicht sehr korrekten höheren Klasse und Mittelklasse wurde das Familienrecht demontiert und angepasst an die Wünsche der sexuellen und relationalen Selbstbestimmer. Das neue Prinzip der individuellen Selbstbestimmung hat das Familienrecht mittlerweile derart subjektiviert, dass von dessen institutionalisierender und symbolisierender Rolle nur noch wenig übrig ist. Das Feld des Rechtes ist immer weniger Ausdruck einer überindividuellen Struktur von nachhaltigen Verhältnissen zwischen Männern, Frauen und Kindern. Hingegen ähnelt das Familienrecht immer mehr einem Werkzeugkasten, womit Bürger – auch dank der medizinischen Biotechnologie – ihre Verwandtschaften und Stammbäume selber basteln können. «[2]

Ich will dieses Zitat nicht in allen Einzelheiten auseinanderlegen und durchbuchstabieren, sondern möchte nur auf einiges hinweisen. So ist das Bild eines Netzwerkes, das wir als Menschen nach eigenen Einsichten zusammenstellen, wohl das vollkommene Gegenteil einer Großfamilie im Schwarzwald, in der die Verhältnisse – und damit die Erwartungen und Verantwortungen – weitgehend festlagen. Auch die Metapher des Familienrechtes als ein »Werkzeugkasten« lässt der Phantasie wenig übrig. Soviel kann man jedenfalls sagen: Das gängige Bild einer geradlinigen Entwicklung zur Befreiung des Individuums wird

[2] Dorien Pessers, Verdwaalde seksen. Over sperminators, metroseksuelen en autocopieën, Annalen van het Thijmgenootschap jaargang 91 (2003) aflevering 4, Nijmegen 2003, 12 (Übersetzung Gerard den Hertog).

hier mindestens nuanciert. Nicht Emanzipation sei die bestimmende Realität, sondern vielmehr neue Herrschaft, und zwar »der sexuellen und relationalen Selbstbestimmer«. Dabei ist vor Augen zu halten, dass Dorien Pessers nicht im »konservativen Lager« zu beheimaten ist, wo man alle Änderungen aus Prinzip mit Argwohn beobachtet.

Im Zitat ist auch die Rede von einer »politisch korrekten« höheren Klasse und Mittelklasse. Damit ist ja gemeint, dass auch in angeblich intellektuellen und unabhängigen Kreisen vor allem oder gar ausschließlich diejenigen Meinungen vorgetragen werden, die in der politischen und gesellschaftlichen Diskussion breite Zustimmung genießen, wobei für nüchterne Fragen und berechtigte Kritik kein Platz ist, obzwar gerade die intellektuelle Debatte für Einwürfe Platz haben sollte und sogar davon lebt! Im Wortlaut von Dorien Pessers lässt sich eine leise Kritik im Blick auf diese Gesellschaftsschicht, der sie auch selber angehört, nicht überhören.

3 *Die Kehrseite*

Es wäre verfehlt, zu meinen, nur diese Gesellschaftsschicht sei wichtig oder bestimme das Bild und die Entwicklungen. Um das vor Augen geführt zu bekommen reicht es, einige Veröffentlichungen des Englischen Psychiaters Theodore Dalrymple zur Kenntnis zu nehmen. Er kennt die Lage in den Unterschichtvierteln der englischen Industriezentren von seiner Berufsperspektive her und zeichnet ein erschütterndes Bild. Er führt aus, wie sich die Meinungen und Auffassungen über Ehe und Sexualität, die seit den sechziger Jahren des vergangenen Jahrhunderts von der Mittelklasse vertreten wurden, ausgewirkt haben. Sexualität sollte – im Namen der wahren Befreiung des Menschen – gelöst werden von allen Einschränkungen in Gestalt von gesellschaftlichen Konventionen oder kirchlichen Vorschriften. Er notiert in ganz trockener Weise, wie die Entkopplung von Sexualität und dauerhafter Beziehung, die bei den Mittelklassen nie vollends in die Tat umgesetzt wurde, inzwischen in der »Unterklasse« »gelandet« ist:

> »Happiness and the good life are conceived as prolonged sensual ecstasy and nothing more.«[3]

[3] Theodore Dalrymple, All sex, all the time, City Journal Summer 2000 (http://www.city-journal.org/html/10_3_urbanities-all_sex.html), auch in:

Derartige Gedanken stehen nicht auf sich. Ihnen liegt ein Bild des Menschen – auch ein unbewusstes oder primitives Bild des Menschen ist ja ein solches! – zu Grunde, in dem das Eigene des Menschen nicht gesucht wird in der Frage, was wirklich gut sei, in der Anerkennung von Grenzen, innerhalb deren die wahre Humanität – und die wahrhaftige Freude – zu finden sei, in einem liebevollen Respekt vor dem Geheimnis im anderen Menschen. Nein,

> »Having been issued the false prospectus of happiness through unlimited sex, modern man concludes, when he is not happy with his life, that his sex has not been unlimited enough. If welfare does not eliminate squalor, we need more welfare; if sex does not bring happiness, we need more sex.«[4]

Die Verwüstung der »Unterseite« der Gesellschaft, wie Dalrymple sie in Zusammenhang mit einer Entkopplung von Sexualität und Lebensbündnis wahrgenommen hat, ist unvorstellbar. Kinder kommen nicht mehr zur Welt in einer stabilen Familie und wachsen darin auch nicht auf. Aus seiner Sicht ist es noch am meisten alarmierend, dass die Ideen jetzt von ›Unten‹ nach ›Oben‹ gehen, dass also die Mittelklasse sich dem Leben und Denken der »Unterklasse« anpasst und ihre Lebensphilosophie – wenn man dieses Wort hierfür verwenden darf – übernimmt.

4 ›Weltfamilienkrise‹

Wenn wir uns noch einen Augenblick das Bild des Bauernhofs im Schwarzwald vor Augen führen, in dem die Linien von der Vergangenheit in die Zukunft sozusagen greifbar da waren und Familie und Verwandtschaft eine Realität darstellten, bedarf es keines Wortes um uns präsent zu machen, welcher Erdrutsch sich hier vollzogen hat. Der Eröffnungssatz des Buches ›The fragmenting family‹ – beachte den Titel! – von Brenda Almond gibt dem Ausdruck:

Theodore Dalrymple, Our Culture, What's Left of It. The Mandarins and the Masses, Chicago 2005, 244.

4 Theodore Dalrymple, All sex, all the time (= Our Culture, What's Left of It. The Mandarins and the Masses, Chicago 2005, 250).

»What is the family? There are many ways of answering this question, but I take as my starting point here G.K. Chestertons's striking metaphor of family as, this frail cord, flung from the forgotten hills of yesterday to the invisible mountains of tomorrow. In more prosaic terms, it is the chain of personal connections that gives meaning to our human notions of past, present and future – a mysterious genetic entity that binds us in our short span of individual existence to our ancestors and to our successors.«[5]

Almond spricht von einer »zerbrechlichen Schnur«, eine »Kette von persönlichen Verbindungen«, die eine »mysteriöse genetische Entität« bildet, die unsere individuelle Existenz verknüpft mit Vorfahren und Nachkommen. Was einmal eine greifbare, allzu greifbare, Realität der Großfamilie war, ist jetzt nur noch blass und zweifelhaft. Es zeigen sich hier weithin Verlust und Verlegenheit und D.S. Brownings Kennzeichnung ›Weltfamilienkrise‹ fällt dem Beobachter leicht wieder ein.

Wie wird dies theologisch wahrgenommen? Was können wir von der Theologie her zur Besinnung auf diese Fragen beitragen? Die Theologie hat sich – in den Niederlanden jedenfalls – weitgehend gefügt in die Entwicklungen, wenn nicht sie begrüßt und theologisch unterbaut und gefördert. Es ist aber Zeit, neu zu fragen und neu zu erwägen.

5 Familie und Verwandtschaft als theologische Themen

Wir sind nicht die ersten, die sich von theologischer Perspektive her mit Familie und Verwandtschaft beschäftigen. Da zeigen sich gleich konfessionelle Unterschiede, zwischen der römisch-katholischen Tradition und dem Protestantismus. Eine mystisch-christologische Begründung der Familie etwa von Johannes 19:27 her – Jesu Worte zu seiner Mutter »Frau, siehe deinen Sohn« und zum Lieblingsjünger »Siehe deine Mutter« – kennen wir Protestanten nicht. In der protestantischen Tradition wird die Familie – das heißt: die Ehe und das Verhältnis zwischen Eltern und Kindern – vor allem vom Dekalog her angegangen. Dabei sind aber im Laufe der Zeit die Unterschiede zwischen der Gesellschaftsordnung, die im Dekalog unterstellt ist, einerseits und unseren in starker Bewegung sich befindlichen Gesellschaften andererseits größer geworden, was nicht ohne Folgen geblieben ist. Die Bibel betrachtet die Familie ja vornehmlich aus

[5] Brenda Almond, The fragmenting family, Oxford 2006, 1.

patriarchaler Perspektive.[6] Heute notiert man mit einer gewissen Verlegenheit, dass unsere moderne Gesellschaft und ihre Sicht von Ehe und Familie sich doch so tiefgreifend von den Strukturen in biblischen Zeiten unterscheidet, dass wir in diesen Fragen die Bibel kaum noch zu hören und zu Rate zu ziehen haben. Dass das fünfte Gebot – »Du sollst deinen Vater und deine Mutter ehren« – keine Legitimierung patriarchaler Gehorsamsverhältnisse ist, sondern Altersfürsorge anordnet, ist den meisten nicht präsent.

6 ›Die Familie im neuen Europa‹

Nun ist in 2008 unter dem Titel ›Die Familie im neuen Europa‹[7] ein Manifest von vier Ethikern – einem römisch-katholischen, einem anglikanischen, einem lutherischen und einem reformierten – erschienen, das in dieser Hinsicht Neuland aufklärt und freilegt. Es zeichnet die Familie als ein Flechtwerk von unterschiedlichen Relationen, in das ein Mensch normalerweise hineingeboren wird. Normalerweise, denn nicht jedem Kind auf dieser Welt wird es zuteil, Eltern, Familie und Verwandtschaft zu haben. Wenn sie noch leben und wir sie kennen, dann üben sie Einfluss auf uns aus, so oder so, so differenziert qua Intensität und manchmal kompliziert es auch ist.

Ist dies romantische Vergangenheit? Nein, die Knechte und Dienstmädchen aus dem Schwarzwald vor einem Jahrhundert sind nicht mehr dabei, es ist kein Zurücksehnen nach einer Lebens- und Arbeitsgemeinschaft aus alten Zeiten. Was ist es dann? Geht es um den Vorrang des Biologischen? Nein, auch das nicht. Adoptiveltern sind auch Eltern, sowie Adoptivkinder auch Kinder ihrer Eltern sind. Dennoch, den biologischen Gesichtspunkt soll man nicht übersehen. Die Fernsehprogramme, in denen Adoptivkinder auf der Suche sind nach ihren Eltern, sind nicht von ungefähr so populär. Das Biologische – wenn ich das so ungeschützt sagen darf – wird im oben genannten Manifest aber in ein bestimmtes Licht hineingestellt. Familienstrukturen

[6] Vgl. z.B. J. M. Vorster, Christian ethical perspectives on marriage and family life in modern Western culture, Hervormde Teologiese Studies 64 (2008) 470.

[7] G. Höver, G.G. de Kruijf, O. O'Donovan & B. Wannenwetsch, Die Familie im neuen Europa. Ethische Herausforderungen und interdisziplinäre Perspektiven, Münster 2008. Seitenangaben zwischen Klammern im laufenden Text.

bilden ein Geflecht, in dem sowohl biologische Verwandtschaften wie auch soziale Verbundenheiten Einfluss auf uns ausüben.[8]

Kennzeichnend für das Manifest ist aus meiner Sicht, dass Identität nicht Endpunkt ist. Bei Dalrymple ist zu lesen, wie eine Glückserfahrung zum innersten Geheimnis der menschlichen Identität wird. Identität ist im Manifest aber nicht Endpunkt, sondern – etwa wie bei Bonhoeffer in seiner Darstellung der »Mandate«[9] – eher der Ort, wo die menschliche Verantwortung Gestalt bekommt. Und wenn es im Menschenleben Glück gibt, dann nicht an dieser Verantwortung vorbei.

Hier sehe ich das Wichtigste dieses Essays. Man setzt sozusagen an der anderen Seite an, nicht bei der Autonomie des Individuums, bei dessen angeblichem Recht, in freier Selbstbestimmung das eigene Leben zu gestalten und auch Beziehungen anzuknüpfen, sondern bei den Verhältnissen die wir vorfinden. Familie und Verwandtschaft bilden – ein Wort von F. de Lange – den »Konvoi womit ein Mensch durch ihr oder sein Leben reist«.[10] Eine der Alternativen, die einem Menschen offenstehen, ist das Anknüpfen einer dauerhaften Beziehung. Der Einsatz bei der Autonomie des individuellen Menschen bestimmt und beschränkt die ethischen Möglichkeiten in hohem Maße. Wenn die menschliche Selbstbestimmung so ungefähr das höchste Gut ist, kommen Eltern und Kinder aus ethischer Perspektive nur in den Blick unter dem Gesichtspunkt der Verantwortung ihnen gegenüber. »Was sind wir ihnen schuldig? « Wo diese Frage leitend ist, da kann die ethische Besinnung sich nicht frei und gestaltend entfalten.

Die Autoren charakterisieren ihren Essay mit dem Ausdruck »askriptiv«. Damit deuten sie an, dass sie die Alternative »deskriptiv« versus »präskriptiv« übersteigen wollen. Die Annäherung an das Thema Familie bzw. Verwandtschaft ist heutzutage oft soziologisch und insofern deskriptiv. Nun ist die soziologische Perspektive ganz wichtig und sie

8 Vgl. auch Brent Waters, The Family in Christian Social and Political Thought, (Oxford Studies in Theological Ethics), Oxford 2007, 206: „Since the family is a human association comprised of biological and social affinities, it is not rooted exclusively in nature or history, but embedded in both. «

9 Vgl. D. Bonhoeffer, Ethik. Herausgegeben von Ilse Tödt, Heinz-Eduard Tödt, Ernst Feil und Clifford Green, DBW Bd. 6, Gütersloh ^{2}1998, 54-60; 392-412; D. Bonhoeffer, Konspiration und Haft 1940-1945, herausgegeben von Jørgen Glenthøj, Ulrich Kabitz und Wolf Krötke. Bearbeitet von Herbert Anzinger, DBW Bd. 16, Gütersloh 1996, 523-527.

10 F. de Lange, Het zwakke gezin, de sterke familie, in: G.G. de Kruijf & P. Schaafsma, Meer dan een optelsom. Kanttekeningen bij de waarde van het gezin, Kampen 2008, 93 (Übersetzung Gerard den Hertog).

darf auch nicht fehlen, vor allem nicht in unserer Zeit, in der soziale Flechtwerke in rapidem Tempo mancherlei Änderungen unterliegen. Wer etwas dazu bemerken möchte, sollte wissen, was dran ist. Eine streng »präskriptive« Annäherung fällt damit aus. Die Autoren des Manifests wollen aber nicht im »Deskriptiven« steckenbleiben. Mit dem Stichwort ›askriptiv‹ plädieren sie für ein »interpretierendes Urteil«, indem man den Entwicklungen auf dem Feld Rechnung trägt und die Dinge in Zusammenhang betrachtet (13).

Die Familie – und mit diesem Wort deuten die Autoren den größeren Lebensverband an, im Unterschied zur Kleinfamilie von Eltern und Kindern – wird eine »Lebensform« genannt. Es geht darin um ein Muster, das man nicht übersehen darf und das sowohl Erwartung als Appell in sich birgt. Es hat denn auch als solches eine bestimmte ethische und theologische Bedeutung. Hier erlernt man gegenseitig füreinander einzustehen.

Die »askriptive« Verantwortung beginnt damit, dass jeder Mensch in ein Flechtwerk von Relationen hineingeboren wird (14).[11] Auch wenn wir alleine im Leben stünden, wie es Überlebenden der Konzentrationslager oder auch von Naturkatastrophen wie auf Haiti passiert ist, wir haben dennoch Eltern, Großeltern, meistens auch Tanten und Onkel, Neffen und Kusinen. Falls wir sie nie gekannt haben, sind sie dennoch als diejenigen, die je gelebt haben, da und tragen sie bei zu unserer Identität. Mein Vater bleibt mein Vater, auch wenn ich ihn nie gekannt habe und inzwischen zweimal so alt bin wie er war, als er starb. Darum wollen Juden, die als einzige Mitglieder einer Familie die Schoah überlebt haben und ihre Familie gar nicht gekannt haben, wissen wer sie alle waren.

Die Familie ist ein »erster Vermittler« (73) unserer Identität, sie ist das »Flussbett«, in das Gott jeden Menschen hineinstellt, wo wir Erfahrungen machen mit menschlicher Existenz zwischen Vergangenheit und Zukunft. Man könnte hier denken an den berühmten Taufbrief Dietrich Bonhoeffers an seinen Neffen Dietrich Bethge[12], in dem er die Familie quasi als eine »Lebensschule der Humanität« (76) darstellt.

11 Vgl. auch Brent Waters, The Family in Christian Social and Political Thought, 179: »We may say that the family is a community *in* which certain integral vocations are embedded, and *from* which they derive their intelligibility.« (Hervorhebung im Text)

12 D. Bonhoeffer, Widerstand und Ergebung. Briefe und Aufzeichnungen aus der Haft. Herausgegeben von Christian Gremmels, Eberhard Bethge und Renate Bethge, in Zusammenarbeit mit Ilse Tödt, DBW Bd. 8, Gütersloh 1998, 428-436.

Nirgends sehen wir klarer, wie das Zusammenleben von Menschen in einander steckt, als in der Familie. Sie ist denn auch nicht ein soziales Konstrukt oder ein Ideal, sondern eine Realität. Sie lässt sich nicht adäquat kennzeichnen als Netzwerk von Beziehungen – viel wesentlicher ist, dass sie selbst Beziehungen generiert (70)! Sie geht der Ehe voraus, wie das fünfte Gebot dem siebten vorangeht (66).

7 Die Konferenz

Es wird klar geworden sein, dass es sich im Thema unserer Konferenz nicht um ein Einzelthema für Spezialisten handelt, sondern dass sich hier bei näherer Betrachtung Grundfragen melden, die uns einladen, wenn nicht drängen, es nicht nur aus ethischer Perspektive, sondern aus gesamttheologischer Perspektive anzugehen. Ich freue mich, dass wir das Thema der Familie oder Verwandtschaft – das in unseren Gesellschaften überall ›dran‹ ist, wenn auch nicht überall auf dieselbe Weise! – auf dieser Konferenz von mehreren Seiten anfassen und diskutieren können. Es steht ja etwas auf dem Spiel, wenn tatsächlich Familie nichts Geringeres ist als eine ganz grundlegende und tief prägende Lebensform und eine Lebensschule der Humanität!

What is at Stake in the Family?

Ethical Reflections on Recent Sociological Research into the Family

Petruschka Schaafsma

1 Family Solidarity is Alive and Well

»The family has wonderfully well withstood the individualistic age«[1]
»The family *is* not bankrupt«[2]
»Intergenerational solidarity alive and well«[3]
»Family solidarity in Europe alive and well«[4]

These are some of the headings used by leading sociologists currently researching the state of the family in Western Europe to introduce their findings in academic publications and popular Dutch media. They ooze a sense of relief: contrary to what most people think, family life is not in decline in West European countries.

I came across these conclusions while looking for recent sociological studies on the state of the family. I am a theological ethicist who deals

1 ›De familie heeft het ik-tijdperk wonderwel doorstaan‹, Opzij, January 2008, 20-22.
2 ›De familie ís niet failliet‹, Trouw, December 24th 2011, 2-3.
3 Tineke Fokkema, Susan ter Bekke, and Pearl A. Dykstra, Solidarity between parents and their adult children in Europe (NiDi report no.76), Amsterdam 2008, 82.
4 Susan ter Bekke and Tineke Fokkema, ›Family Solidarity in Europe Alive and Well‹, Demos, Bulletin over Bevolking en Samenleving (NiDi) special edition 24/2008, 8-10.

with the topic of the family. As such, it is important to be informed about current scientific social research and literature on the actual situation of the family. The conclusions are striking, for several reasons. First of all, their reassuring tone seems to reflect a polemic: Were these studies intended to contradict views that are apparently prevalent in today's society, i.e. views of ›family pessimists' who despair at the future of the family? I wondered if this polemic was addressed explicitly in the studies and if advocates and opponents referred to the same facts. A normative discussion about the nature and status of the present-day family, a discussion about what the family means and should mean, seemed to be presupposed here. Moreover, such a discussion was claimed to be relevant for society. However, that this discussion was not presented as a normative, but as a merely ›factual‹ discussion, looked evident. How would this work out?

I was struck by the conclusions secondly because the appearance of the term ›solidarity‹ in this context of the family was not immediately clear to me, an outsider to family sociology. My dictionary confirms my thought that ›solidarity‹ is about supporting people or groups of people who are in trouble and need of help. People in a distant country struck by natural disaster are an example. So are exploited people from a professional group not my own. Showing solidarity in these contexts signifies a conscious act of becoming related to a group of people in a visible way, e.g. by public demonstration, or in a practical way, e.g. by sending money. Before solidarity is shown, one does not have any explicit relation or practical connection to these people. Solidarity is an *ad hoc* connection. I was at first unable relate these meanings to the context of the family, as the family is characterised by precisely the opposite: family is characterised by a permanent, certain, and, in a sense, natural connection. What would the term ›solidarity‹ mean in the family context? Why would it be the focus of these studies?

In this article, I take these two strands of ›outsider‹ questions as a starting point for a further exploration of recent sociological studies from a theological ethical perspective. The outsider perspective gives rise to criticism, which may be for the larger part a result of my unfamiliarity with family sociology. My aim is not to alert sociologists to the gaps in their research: my aim is to find out how I can make fruitful use of the questions their studies raise in an ethical investigation. Reading these studies may reveal appropriate directions for theological ethical analysis. This would be of particular importance in my native Dutch context, where these empirical studies are a dominant source for the development of policy. I do not aim to give a complete overview of current family sociology. No, I will focus on some recent, large-scale Western European studies on family solidarity with a prominent presence in current public debate. I will start by exploring the meaning of solidarity in these studies and the reasons these studies give for their focus on this topic. I will follow up by discussing the most important outcomes of this research. I will also discuss how these findings are thought to further the understanding of the current situation of widespread concern about the family. In discussing these studies, the outlines of a proper approach from a theological ethical perspective will become visible.

2 Focus on Solidarity

In the first decade of the present century, a large sociological research project on the current state of the family was initiated in the Netherlands and funded by the Netherlands Organization for Scientific Research (NWO), as part of a European programme.[5] The key concept of this ›Netherlands Kinship Panel Study‹ (NKPS) is family solidarity, which is defined as ›feelings of mutual affinity in family relationships‹ and the expression thereof ›in behavioural terms‹, ›such as contact and support‹.[6] In the same period, similar studies can be found based on data from various European countries.[7] Many of these solidarity studies are

5 The programme is called ›Netherlands Kinship Panel Study‹ (NKPS) and is part of the UN Generations and Gender Programme: ›a system of nationally comparative surveys and contextual databases, which aims at improving the knowledge base for policy making in countries of the United Nations Economic Commission for Europe‹. It is a large longitudinal study consisting of three waves (wave 1 in 2002-2004, wave 2 in 2006-2007, wave 3 in 2010-2011). The data were and are collected from both structured interviews and in-depth open interviews with individual respondents as well as family members. Cf. www.nkps.nl (accessed 1/19/12).

6 Pearl A. Dykstra, Matthijs Kalmijn, Trudie C.M. Knijn, Aafke E. Komter, Aart C. Liefbroer, and Clara H. Mulder, Family Solidarity in the Netherlands, Amsterdam 2006, 15; this page refers to the NKPS codebook (P.A. Dykstra et al., Codebook of the Netherlands Kinship Panel Study: A multi-actor, multimethod panel study on solidarity in family relationships. Wave 1. NKPS Working Paper No. 4., The Hague 2005, 11).

7 Cf. e.g. the studies by Svein Daatland and Katharina Herlofson in four European countries and Israel (S.O. Daatland and K. Herlofson, ›»Lost Solidarity« or »Changed Solidarity«: A Comparative European View of Normative Family Solidarity‹, Ageing and Society, 23/2003, 537-60); publications related to the 2004 survey in 11 European countries ›Survey of Health, Ageing and Retirement

good examples of family research that explicitly takes as its starting point the intuition that the family is in decline. The research is supposed to lead to a conclusion on the correctness of this intuition. Thus, the NKPS' starting point is that ›the family is not what it used to be‹ and that ›family relationships have undergone a dramatic transformation‹ in the past few decades.[8] This transformation is visible in three fields.[9]

Firstly, partner relationships have changed, particularly because of increased female participation in the labour force. Partners interact and communicate differently and the form of the relationship is more a matter of choice. For that matter, so is having a relationship at all.

Secondly, relationships between parents and children are described as more equal and more intimate. The trend of leaving home at ever younger ages seems to have halted. Due to increasing divorce rates, increasing numbers of parents do not live with their young children any more.

Finally, relationships with family members outside the household are changing. Families verticalize, narrowing horizontally. This results in a so-called ›beanpole shape‹, in increasing geographical distances and in the participation of the adult children in the labour force. Moreover, support in general and to elderly parents in particular is no longer regarded as a self-evident family duty.

The NKPS investigates whether these developments lead to a ›decline in solidarity within family relationships‹ and an ›erosion of family bonds‹. It also investigates the consequences to a person's functioning in society, social cohesion and inequality. Factual information on these topics is seen as ›essential for framing policies to safeguard the solidarity the family helps to provide‹.[10] Solidarity is thus immediately introduced as something at risk, something that used to be self-evident but is now in danger of being lost.[11] Research should examine the correctness of this assumption. We are in the midst of a debate heavily charged with connotations of traditionalism and

in Europe (SHARE)‹, e.g., Fokkema et al., Solidarity between Parents and their Adult Children.

8 Dykstra et al., Family Solidarity in the Netherlands, 11, 14.

9 Dykstra et al., Family Solidarity in the Netherlands, 11-14.

10 Dykstra et al., Family Solidarity in the Netherlands, 14.

11 For a brief critical discussion of these suggestions cf. H. Bertram, ›Die Familie: Solidarität oder Individualität?‹, in: Leszlo A. Vaskovics (ed.), Familienbilder und Familienrealitäten, Opladen 1997.

progressivism. Are things getting worse or are they changing for the better?

The focus on the concept of solidarity often goes unaccounted for in research. It is rather taken for granted that an investigation into the present state of the family would focus on this issue. Occasionally brief references to the history of the term's use are found. History confirms that the term is related to a normative discussion, which weighs the great life pattern changes in the twentieth century.

Émile Durkheim (1858-1917) and Ferdinand Tönnies (1855-1936) are the founding fathers of the sociological focus on solidarity.[12] They used the term ›solidarity‹ to make sense of the great changes taking place in society as a result of the Industrial Revolution[13]: roles and occupations varied increasingly, and people were connected primarily on the basis of instrumental, functional relationships. Durkheim and Tönnies wondered what the specific nature and basis of the new social order would be. Solidarity is used in this context as a term particularly indicating the basis of the social order.[14] Both Durkheim and Tönnies distinguish between old or traditional and new or modern forms of solidarity. Durkheim calls the traditional cohesion ›mechanical solidarity‹, whereas Tönnies call it *Gemeinschaft*. The traditional cohesion is characterised by strong bonds based on shared norms and customs. A result of the Industrial Revolution is that people became dependent on one another in different ways. Instead of shared norms, division of labour binds people together, resulting in an ›organic solidarity‹ (Durkheim), a *Gesellschaft* (Tönnies) in which relations are based on consensus or contract instead of being based on normative obligations. Later theorists specified this binary distinction further by identifying the relevant bases of group solidarity. In line with the

12 Robert E.L. Roberts, Leslie N. Richards, & Vern L. Bengtson, ›Intergenerational Solidarity in Families: Untangling the Ties That Bind‹, Marriage and Family Review 16/1991, 11-46, 11-15, 20; Aafke E. Komter & Wilma A.M. Vollebergh, ›Solidarity in Dutch Families: Family Ties Under Strain?‹, Journal of Family Issues 23/2 2002, 171-88, 171-73.

13 The primary works that are mentioned are: E. Durkheim, The Division of Labour in Society (De La Division Du Travail Social), 1893 and F. Tönnies, Community and Society (Gemeinschaft und Gesellschaft) 1887. Cf. Lamanna's critical remark that references to Durkheim in family sociology are only ›tangential‹ and do not ›provide a firm fix‹ on the family sociology that is in fact a substantial part of Durkheim's work (Mary Ann Lamanna, Emile Durkheim on the Family, Thousand Oaks 2002, 3).

14 Roberts et al., ›Intergenerational Solidarity in Families‹, 12.

theories developed by Durkheim and Tönnies, they distinguished between internalised normative prescriptions, functional interdependencies, and consensus between members on rules of exchange.[15]

In the 1950s and 1960s social psychologists further developed the theory of solidarity. George Homans developed a classic distinction, which was extended by Fritz Heider. Homans and Heider distinguished between collective activities or interaction, functional interdependence, mutual affection, shared norms on group behaviour, and similarity or consensus in a more general sense.[16] These are general theories, applying to all kinds of groups. However, *family* sociologists subsequently tried to identify the specific characteristics of *family* solidarity from these general theories in such a way that they could also be measured in empirical research. The aspects of solidarity they identified were largely similar to those generally characterising solidarity in groups.[17] The specific patterns of solidarity that characterise the family would then become clear by way of the relations between these aspects. The hypothesis was that, in the family, normative solidarity would be primary in the sense that it determines affection, association, and contact. Strongly normative views on family relationships would be able to overcome divergent values. Such dissension seemed likely to occur given the coexistence of different generations. The precise content of these characteristic family norms is not described, however. One only finds very general formulations like ›the more parents and children believe

15 Roberts et al., ›Intergenerational Solidarity in Families‹, 15.

16 Roberts et al., ›Intergenerational Solidarity in Families‹, 15; Komter et al., ›Solidarity in Dutch Families‹, 173.

17 Many current family sociological studies on solidarity (e.g., Daatland et al., ›»Lost Solidarity« or »Changed Solidarity«‹; Dykstra et al, Family solidarity in the Netherlands, 123-124; Fokkema et al., Solidarity between Parents and their Adult Children, 4-5) mention the six dimensions of solidarity as developed by Robert Roberts, Leslie Richards, Vern Bengtson (cf. note 12 above). The technical terms for these dimensions are: associational solidarity (how and how often family members interact), affectual solidarity (type and degree of feelings of affections), consensual solidarity (degree of consensus on values, etc.), functional solidarity (degree of exchange of help/services), normative solidarity (perception and enactment of norms of family solidarity), and the family structure (size, geographical proximity, etc.). Claude Martin indicates two relatively distinct periods in the emergence of the concept of family solidarity in French sociological research. In the 1960s and 1970s, family solidarity was studied in relation to kinship ties, while from 1985-1995 family solidarity became a theme of its own, also in public debate (Claude Martin, ›The Rediscovery of Family Solidarity‹, in: Trudie Knijn and Aafke Komter (eds), Solidarity between the Sexes and the Generations. Transformation in Europe, Cheltenham 2004, 3-17).

they *should* love, visit and help one another, the more they will actually do so.‹[18] Normativity seems to refer to some notion of obligation to maintain contact and exchange help, the obligation to show solidarity.[19]

This idea of an obligation to help is in some way inexplicitly regarded as the core of the normative solidarity of the family. This is confirmed by hints at problematic aspects of traditional family life of which we are nowadays happily freed. Daatland and Herlofson argue that ›... as families were almost entirely responsible for elder care before the welfare state, it is reasonable to assume that increased formal services have been welcomed by younger and older generations. When alternatives are available, today's older people seem more reluctant to receive help from the family than are adult children willing to provide such help, and the young are *more* inclined towards family care provision than the old‹.[20]

The exchange of help within the family apparently is a controversial issue in present-day society. Komter and Vollebergh mention that, contrary to relations of friendship, the exchange between family members is based primarily on involuntary obligation instead of feelings of affection. They regard this phenomenon as problematic, because it may evoke ›feelings of dependency‹ which people prefer to avoid.[21] Knijn and Komter also describe family solidarity as being at odds with

18 Roberts et al., ›Intergenerational Solidarity in Families‹, 23 (emphasis mine).

19 The importance of norms as regards family obligations is underlined because they serve in the research as a predictor of actual help (Fokkema et al., Solidarity between Parents and Their Adult Children, 35). Moreover it is important in people's evaluation of family relations, because it indicates what may be expected from these relations (Dykstra et al., Family Solidarity in the Netherlands, 123). Still, these obligations are formulated in a very general way. As an example, I will quote the four central statements that were part of a questionnaire into family solidarity. Participants in the research were asked to indicate their agreement with the following statements: 1. Adult children should live close to their older parents so that they can help them if needed; 2. Adult children should be willing to sacrifice some of the things they want for their own children in order to support their frail elderly parents; 3. Older people should be able to depend on their adult children to help them do the things they need to do; 4. Parents are entitled to some return for the sacrifices they have made for their children (Daatland et al., ›»Lost Solidarity« or »Changed Solidarity«‹, 543). In sum, solidarity is about staying close to one's parents and helping them even if this means making sacrifices. The only substantial background for this obligation of adult children to help their parents is expressed in the fourth remark: it is an economic rationale, one pays one's parents back (›return‹) for the latter's efforts.

20 Daatland et al., ›»Lost Solidarity« or »Changed Solidarity«‹, 556.

21 Komter et al., ›Solidarity in Dutch Families‹, 186.

›individual family members' need for autonomy‹.[22] Dykstra and Komter indicate that public opinion is divided as to the evaluation of the fact that providing support to family members has increasingly become a matter of choice. They analyse this debate as one between advocates and opponents of the process of individualisation.[23] All these remarks on the controversial status of family obligation to support and care are, however, incidental and appear mostly in the introductory parts; there is no further elaboration on, for example, why norms and obligations on family contact and the giving and receiving of help have become problematic in our time.

From the outsider's ethical perspective, the most striking issue with this focus on solidarity is this: that the research operates on a specific idea of what characterises family bonds in comparison to other ties, which is hardly accounted for. This lack of clarification with respect to the initial ideas or working definitions is repeated in the notion of ›family solidarity‹. The specific aspects of solidarity that are investigated are not compared to or justified over and against other possible sets of aspects.[24] Solidarity does not have the usual connotation of conscious ad hoc support, but has become a technical term, taken for granted as an important sociological category. The value of this term as a focus for the investigation of the current state of the family is explained nor justified.

3 Conclusions: Reassuring, but about What?

The undertones of ›dramatic transformation‹ and concerns about possible declines in family solidarity are found more often in studies at the end of the twentieth century and the beginning of the twenty-first than in the early family sociology of the 1950s. In the latter category I found examples of fairly open research into, e.g. the categories by means of which solidarity can be assessed, their interrelationship, the predictors of family solidarity, and the consequences of such solidarity, i.e., the question of whether its effects are positive or harmful.[25] Some of

22 Knijn et al., Solidarity between the Sexes and the Generations, xxi.

23 Dykstra et al., Family Solidarity in the Netherlands, 13, 14.

24 Cf. the six characteristics formulated by Bengtson and Schrader. This taxonomy is often adopted without discussing other possible parameters.

25 Studies that formulate their aims without a worried undertone are, e.g., Luther T. Jansen, ›Measuring Family Solidarity‹, American Sociological Review 17/6 1952, 727-33; Ivan Nye & William Rushing, ›Toward Family Measurement

the most important results of research in this category are that there is support for the idea that strong norms on family obligations contribute to affection, contact, and the exchange of help between parents and adult children. It was also found that greater opportunities for interaction promote contact whereas constraints such as geographical distance injure levels of contact.[26]

However, more recent research wants to find out if solidarity is in danger. Perhaps the concern reflected in this research may be parallel to that at the end of the nineteenth century. This is suggested by Komter and Vollebergh. In both ›fin de siècle‹ periods, great changes loomed: new societal structures cause primarily by the division of labour at the end of the nineteenth, or phenomena like individualization, the erosion of traditional structures and morals, urbanization, the increase in mobility, globalisation, higher levels of education, and so on at the end of the twentieth century.[27] The more recent research, done in a variety of West European countries, explicitly rejects the suggestion that solidarity and the family in general are in decline:

- ›Family bonds remain supremely important in our modern society.‹[28]
- ›»Solidarity change« more accurately summarizes contemporary opinion and behaviour than »solidarity lost«. The adaptability of solidarity to change may be a key to the strength and persistence of family relationships.‹[29]
- ›[O]ur conclusions ... do not indicate in any way that the family is in decline. The assumption that the individualization process diminishes loyalty towards and identification with family members ... was not borne out by our data.‹[30]
- ›[O]ur findings do not indicate at all that the structural and cultural

Research‹, in: Jeffrey K. Hadden and Marie L. Borgatta, Marriage and the Family, Itasca, Ill. 1969, 133-40; Roberts et al., ›Intergenerational Solidarity in Families‹; Vern L. Bengtson and Robert E.L. Roberts, ›Intergenerational Solidarity in Aging Families: An Example of Formal Theory Construction‹, Journal of Marriage and Family 53/4 1991, 856-70.

26 Roberts et al., ›Intergenerational Solidarity in Families‹, 37; Bengtson et al., ›Intergenerational Solidarity in Aging Families‹ 867-868.

27 Komter et al., ›Solidarity in Dutch Families‹, 171.

28 Komter et al., ›Solidarity in Dutch Families‹, 186.

29 Daatland et al., ›»Lost Solidarity« or »Changed Solidarity«‹, 557.

30 Dykstra et al., Family Solidarity in the Netherlands, 154.

changes in European families have resulted in a decline in actual intergenerational solidarity.‹[31]

These conclusions are based on facts that indicate, most importantly, that parent-child relationships remain strong. There is frequent contact: at least one child lives close to the parents, there are strong ›family care obligations‹, especially on the part of older parents for their children and grandchildren, and there is a brisk exchange of help.[32] A trend that confirms the idea that family life has changed is the fact that not all family members live in close proximity, particularly in case of highly educated people. Highly educated people have less family contact than people with a lower education. Education levels aside, there are differences between European countries, especially between the more individualistic northern and the more family-oriented southern countries.[33] Nevertheless, norms obliging adult children to care for their elderly parents in a substantial way prevail in societies with a strong welfare state, too.[34] The conclusion is that solidarity still exists, even though its expressions are changing. The welfare state may influence the forms solidarity takes, it does not abolish the obligation to care or help as such.[35]

31 Fokkema et al., Solidarity between Parents and their Adult Children, 82. The authors add that this conclusion ›confirms the most common conclusion of previous studies (e.g. Attias-Donfut & Wolff, 2000; Chappell & Blandford, 1991; Daatland, 1992; Daatland & Herlofson, 2003a, 2003b; Hank, 2007; Tomassini *et al.*, 2004b).‹ The difference from these studies is that the SHARE investigation is based on 11 different European countries and focuses on different dimensions of solidarity.

32 Fokkema et al., Solidarity between Parents and their Adult Children, 83; Dykstra et al., Family Solidarity in the Netherlands, 154.

33 Fokkema et al., Solidarity between Parents and their Adult Children, 87.

34 Daatland et al., ›»Lost Solidarity« or »Changed Solidarity«‹, 556-57. In a comparison between the situation in the Netherlands and the USA, Teresa M. Cooney and Pearl A. Dykstra conclude that the likelihood of intergenerational support is higher in the Netherlands than in the USA, whereas public provisions are more generous in the former than in the latter country (›Family Obligations and Support Behaviour: A United States-Netherlands Comparison‹, Ageing and Society 31, 2011, 1026-50, 1044-5).

35 ›[A]cross Europe today strong and stable normative family solidarity co-exists with changing personal preferences and policy recommendations for care. ‹Solidarity is observed to be something that can adapt itself to new situations, and it is therefore recommended as a focus for further research into the family as well (Daatland et al, ›»Lost Solidarity« or »Changed Solidarity«‹, 558 (referring to Finch & Mason 1990, 1993)).

The undertone of relief and reassurance is hard to miss. As the outcomes relate to the popular, supposedly widespread opinion of ›family decline‹, there is something triumphant in these conclusions as well: the popular view can be contradicted. In spite of their firm character, these results do not leave me, an outsider, assured. The claim that the research can cast light on a topical and controversial issue gives rise to several questions.

First of all, one wonders why there is such concern about the family. Is this characteristic of our times? Could it be common in all times? The research did not take the form of a historical comparison, nor did it answer the question of what is at stake in the issue of the family in our times. To answer this question, it would be helpful to know how people determine who belongs to the family these days. Is blood relationship the most prominent factor? Or is being a family perceived much more as a matter of *consciously* relating oneself to others in an intimate and, in principle, lasting bond? And is the distinction between familial and other relationships actually important in determining choices and behaviour, or do we interact with family members and friends or neighbours in a similar way? The research on solidarity suggests that family relationships are of a specific kind, and that the specific character of family solidarity gives insight in what characterises family relationships in comparison to other relationships. But, in the end, the conclusions focus more on the prevalence of family solidarity than on its precise content. Thus, it is not clear what exactly we possess in this family solidarity. It is presented as a good, so we should be happy that it is still there. On the other hand, the only characteristic with which it was described was an obligation to help and support. This obligation was also referred to as a controversial thing, which would indicate that family solidarity is not a straightforward good.

In sum, this complex of unanswered questions relates to the factual meaning of the family in our times. Since this meaning is not clarified, it is difficult to see how the conclusions address ›widespread concerns‹ in a relevant way. However, the impression that the solidarity researchers suppose their results disprove such concerns is hard to avoid.

4 A Theological Contribution

Reflection on the research on solidarity from an ethical perspective indicates a field that is still unexplored. It is necessary to explore this field in order to address the family issue as it is now present in society. This is the field roughly outlined by the relationship between family and certain obligations to help and care. How can ethical reflection and, in particular, reflection nourished by a theological background, contribute to understanding in this field?

In my view, the risk of any ethical approach, a theological one in particular, is that its normative character is understood primarily in the prescriptive sense of defining what a good family is. Such an approach would specify whether divorce or cohabitation is allowed, etc. Many family ethics result in a plea for so-called ›traditional‹ family life. I think a different though no less concrete kind of normative reflection is needed. This reflection would principally aim to discover what is at stake in the family issue, why the phenomenon of the family has become a subject of concern, and which accompanying meanings make the issue difficult. To find out what is at stake was the exact reason for my turning to the sociological studies. However, the approach these studies took raised many questions for me as an outsider. Therefore, my own reflection on these studies put me on track of this different, ethical approach. In closing, I would like to outline the focus of such an ethical approach.

Family relationships were suggested to be characterised by particular norms. The scarce remarks about the content of these norms focused more on the obligation to extend help and care than on the situation of receiving it. In spite of the brisk exchanges of help that were observed between family members, there were hints that this exchange was problematic because of its obligatory character and the dependence it implicated. Dependence was seen as an important and controversial implication of help and care as such. This was explained by referring to the modern emphasis on independence, autonomy and free choice of what one deems important. In recent ethics, reflection on the tension between the modern view of humans in control of their own lives and the reality of vulnerability and dependency has been taken up especially in care ethics.[36] But what interests us here is why care would be controversial precisely in the context of the family. What does this context add to the general problem of giving and receiving help and care and the problems of an obligation to care and becoming dependent? To answer this question, further ethical reflection is needed on the specific

[36] I will mention a single important title in this respect: Eva Feder Kittay and Ellen K. Feder, The Subject of Care: Feminist Perspectives on Dependency, Oxford 2002.

character of the family relationship in comparison to other relationships and why this has become a topic of discussion nowadays.

The analysis of present-day relationships by sociologist Anthony Giddens may indicate the direction such a reflection would take. Giddens argues that, at present, equality, voluntarism, openness, and a basis in sympathy or love have become central values by which we, particularly in the West, assess relationships and decide on their continuation.[37] Family relationships are also modelled on this ideal. As a result, the family is built around the couple, the relationship that most easily matches this ideal. Relationships to other family members are subordinated to it.[38] Giddens regards this as a development that has to be valued positively: the ›democracy of the emotions in everyday life ... is just as important as public democracy in improving the quality of our lives‹.[39] This normative statement, unsubstantiated by Giddens, raises several questions. Is there nothing in the family that resists the very focus of this model? Is it possible to simply leave behind all ›given‹, non-chosen aspects of family life by concentrating on the couple? Would the intergenerational character not imply a principal inequality that, in a sense, never disappears as one gets older? Does not the idea of a lasting alliance somehow stick to the family, the idea of something not primarily subject to being shaped or controlled by the individual?

Aspects such as these are difficult to envisage and value in Giddens' framework of a democracy of the emotions. The same is true for the ›obligations to help and care‹ that distinguish family bonds from other bonds. These seem to be obligations of a specific kind: they would have the connotation of being self-evident and independent of, e.g. the quality of the relationship. They are ›given‹, much like family relationships themselves are ›given‹, instead of assumed voluntarily. Moreover, this obligation to help and care may place great demands on people. It may even amount to self-sacrifice. If the solidarity research is correct in stating that such relations of help and care are currently prevalent among family members in spite of their controversial nature, the need to clarify this aspect of ›self-evident care‹ is all the more pressing. One should also ask if the language of ›obligation‹ is the best way to express and clarify

37 Anthony Giddens, Runaway World. How Globalization is Reshaping our Lives, London, 2002^2, Chapter 4 ›Family‹ (pp. 51-66).

38 Giddens describes this as ›the rise of the couple and coupledom‹ (Runaway World, 59).

39 Giddens, Runaway World, 63.

what happens in the family situation.[40] By dealing with these issues, one would gain insight into the meaning of current family life.

I would like to conclude by indicating what asking these questions from a theological perspective may contribute to these reflections. Because of its familiarity with religion, a theological perspective implies a somewhat uncomfortable relationship towards modernity. A theological perspective would thus, in general, strengthen the critical evaluation of the current ›democratic‹ view on relationships and the view on man that supports it. A more specific question that theology would raise is what light the relationship of human beings to the transcendent, or to God, casts on relationships between humans, particularly those between family members. To answer this question in the context of a Western theological ethics that operates with reference to Jewish and Christian religious sources in particular, one would have to make sense of the striking observation that family relationships play a central role in biblical imagery, especially in depicting the relationship between God and his people or the believer. Thus, biblical texts are an important field for exploring the possible meanings of family in a context in which family is more self-evident than ours. Analysing this imagery would provide us with mirror views to which we can hold up and compare our own meanings to clarify them. An obvious meaning this imagery would put forward is that the relationship between God and human beings is never a completely equal one, and thus seems fundamentally at odds with our ›democratic‹ views on relationships. It would be important to analyse the meanings and values connected with this ›unequal‹ relationship. Another aspect may be that of God's

40 From the 1980s onwards, ethicists have invoked precisely the context or moral practice of the family to critique the one-sided focus on the modern rights/duties-based ethics, the corresponding Enlightenment views of human beings as free, autonomous individuals – translated into liberal political philosophy – as well as the claim to universality that accompanies many of these metaethical theories. The criticisms come down to the statement that this focus does not correspond to actual moral practice, like that of the family (cf. e.g., Christina Hoff Sommers, ›Filial Morality‹, The Journal of Philosophy, 83/1986, 439-56; id., ›Philosophers against the Family‹, in: G. Graham and H. Lafollette (eds), Person to Person, Philadelphia: Temple University Press 1989, 82-105). Family may be pre-eminently a context in which the questions of rights and obligations, of ›what I get and what I am due do not loom large‹ (Michael Sandel, Liberalism and the Limits of Justice, Cambridge 1982, 33). Hume is often invoked as the founding father of a different kind of ethics, that disappeared, however, behind the dominant views of Kant and Mill (cf. the work of Annette Baier).

faithfulness to believers, which is often presented as stronger than the believer's infidelity, as overruling it. Finally, dependence upon God seems to be a fundamental characteristic of the relationship between God and the believer. Aspects like those of inequality, indissolubility, and dependence immediately strike us as strange or troublesome in the context of relationships. The biblical literature provides us with texts to discover what they may mean in a framework of meanings and values different from that of our time.

The aim of exploring these unfamiliar meanings would not be to restore some pre-modern constellation. Its aim would be to understand and appropriate meanings that have become difficult in modernity and therefore provide insight into modernity. The family, then, offers a wonderful opportunity to study our laborious relation to modernity, a relation in which we are no longer at home but that we cannot simply forget or leave behind. Theology may help us to find an outsider's perspective that provides us with the estrangement necessary for such a critical project.

Families in Ancient Israel

Society, Economy, Religion

Előd Hodossy-Takács

1 Introduction

Today's devoted Christians endeavour to live according to biblical ethical standards stemming from early Christian traditions. Or at least I hope they do. Christians do not treat divorce as a mere legal question, they either live alone or in a monogamous marriage, they avoid sexual relationships with close family members, etc. Most of these things resemble New Testament ethical ideas.

However, the Old Testament picture of families is different. In the Hebrew Bible we are faced with polygamous families, while among the patriarchs a marriage with the »women of the land« (Gen 27:46) raised a damning voice. Endogamy was practised: young men took their wives from within the clan. These passages along with Torah teachings such as accepting gifts as a compensation for the loss of a daughter's workforce, or marrying captive women (Deut 20:10–14), provide evidence of just how distant the ancient understanding of the family is from our own social behaviour.

There are both similarities and differences between the social order of the Old Testament times and our era. The most important similarity is the existence of families. To this day the family is a central institution, like it was in Ancient Near Eastern societies. Using this statement as a point of departure, we can list some variation. The position of men and women in society and in the family structure is probably the most striking difference. Ancient people did not think of themselves as individuals, but they considered themselves as persons within a family unit. »The family was a social, economic, legal and religious entity that bound its members in a series of mutual obligations.«[1]

2 *Families within the framework of the ancient Israelite social system*

As early as the mid-second millennium BC, Near Eastern households and expanded families were bound together by a complex structure of agreements, with the intention to ensure the well-being and security of each community member. These agreements fixed the grades of dependency and the modes of decision-making, they defined the status of men, women and children as well as the laws of inheritance and the keeping of the memory of the deceased.

Groups of nuclear families cooperated economically as well. Since all of them were involved in the same agricultural or productive activities, they worked together, and cooperatively hired additional workforce on a temporal or permanent basis, etc.

Laws also guarded the family's integrity.[2] The Code of Hammurabi deals extensively with the law of domestic relations, to which 68 paragraphs out of a total of 282 are devoted.

In the Hebrew Bible the most important texts regarding family life were sometimes written as lengthy narratives,[3] though interesting passages may also be found in the legal material found in Exodus and Deuteronomy. Other passages are found dispersed throughout the prophetic books.[4] Although these texts contain large amounts of relevant material it remains impossible to describe Israelite family life from the Bible alone. The fundamental problem is the background of the authors – they were scribes, city dwellers, and literate males. As such they did not represent ordinary people, and ordinary families. The absolute majority, the illiterate, the peasants, craftsmen and women[5] remain mute,

1 Gerald L. Mattingly, Family. In: Piotr Bienkowski, Piotr and Alan Millard (eds.), Dictionary of the Ancient Near East (DANE), Philadelphia 2000, 113.
2 Gerald L. Mattingly, Family, 114.
3 E.g. the stories of the matriarchs and patriarchs in Genesis; the case of Micah's household in Judges, etc. For Micah see the informative chapter in P.J. King and L.E. Stager, Life in Biblical Israel, Louisville 2001, 9-19.
4 E.g. the case of Jeremiah and the Rechabites, Jer 35.
5 Susan Ackerman, Digging Up Deborah. Near Eastern Archaeology (NEA). 66/4, Dec 2003, 172-184.

unnamed, and largely silenced in the text. However, archaeological findings and material remains reveal something of their lives.

Structure

Though we find overlaps and inconsistencies in biblical Hebrew terminology, the unit terms of the hierarchy are, generally speaking: ›people‹, ›tribe‹, ›clan‹, ›house‹, and ›male individual‹.[6] We are currently concerned with the last three.

The *men* are those frequently addressed as *you*, a term which implies more than adult males. As Timothy Willis states: »A man's wife, children and ... slaves ... are considered as part of the man or [an] extension of the man in legal matters. They are one with the man, but each has the potential to separate from him. ... This sense of oneness represents their basic understanding of family.«[7] Accepting this view the term would denote about the same as today's nuclear family.

A *house* is an extended families, a unit sometimes sociologically difficult to discern from *clans*. Both units are lineage groups: the extended families lived together, very often in the same household or in attached buildings, and the clans were also arranged on the same territory. *Clans* had an important legal role: the practice of family solidarity took place within these units. Briefly, the clans and the extended families were visible, effective and socially, economically and legally active units of people related to one another.[8]

In early Israelite society the extended family and the clan were the most prominent forms of social organization. The levels above the clan, namely the tribe and the nation were not functional but literary units.[9] This overall picture is widely accepted as relevant for the so-called early Israel (1200-1000 BC).

6 'am (עַם), sebet (שֵׁבֶט), mispachah (מִשְׁפָּחָה), bet 'ab (בֵּית־אָב) / bayit (בַּיִת), geber (גֶּבֶר) / 'is (אִישׁ). Josh 7:14. See the entries in: W.A. VanGemeren (ed.), New International Dictionary of Old Testament Theology and Exegesis (NIDOTTE) I-V, Carlisle 1996. [esp. vol. 2. 1140.] Timothy M. Willis, Clan, The New Interpreter's Dictionary of the Bible (NIDB) vol. 1. 679.

7 Timothy M. Willis, Family. NIDB 2,427-48

8 The Hebrew term mispachah occurs about 300 times in the OT, but only in 170 cases it is translated as ›clan‹. About the inconsistencies see NIDOTTE 2, 1141.

9 K van der Toorn, Family Religion in Babylonia, Syria and Israel. Continuity and Change in the Forms of Religious Life, Leiden 1996, 194-205.

In my opinion, the role of the extended family remained similar during the Israelite monarchy to the situation in the early Iron Age.[10] This holds true for the clans as well: although they lost their military function, they remained intact in matters of solidarity. Many readers of the Bible are tempted to believe that the transition to the monarchy caused an enormous change in the social organization of the Israelite people. Without entering into particulars, I have to state that the transition to the monarchy did not create such a momentous shift in family life. The dwellings that appear for the first time in Iron Age I strata, which Biblically speaking lies in the period of the judges, remained typical during the monarchy as well. The same goes for the most important methods of agricultural production. The standards of living in both periods are practically identical. As there was only a limited amount of urbanization in Palestine, their everyday activities remained the same.[11] Why would we expect a dramatic change in family life just because a king, a figure who remained distant from the ordinary people, moved into prominence in Jerusalem?

On the other hand, the rise of the kingship indeed created economic changes and therefore had consequences for the entire social structure. Forced labour, central administration, monumental building projects and crown property all affected family life. Society however remained almost exclusively agricultural in nature, even though taxation and the temporary burden of working outside of the family fields created tensions. In the words of V. Fritz: »the establishment of the monarchy meant an economic burden for the Israelite farmer, since now a part of the agricultural production had to be given to the crown.« [12] This was compensated by more secure markets. In certain cases this compensation was not enough, and debt and slavery were the consequences.

Visibility – the four-room house

The most common dwellings in Iron Age Israel were the so called four-room houses. These houses were built around a central, paved area. Two rows of pillars separated the side rooms from the central space; the

10 Robert R. Wilson, family, the. In: P.J. Achtemeier (ed.), Harper's Bible Dictionary, San Francisco 1985, 302-303.

11 According to social scientists every pre-industrial society was 90% non-urban! Carol Meyers, The Family in Early Israel. In: L.G. Perdue, and J. Blenkinsopp (eds.), Families in Ancient Israel, Louisville, 1997, 6.

12 V. Fritz, The City in Ancient Israel, Sheffield 1995, 174 (see 160-175).

fourth room was behind the central space. The terminology is misleading, since the ›four rooms‹ only denote the common division of the ground level and ignore the upper story and subdivisions downstairs, as the owners frequently turned large rooms into smaller spaces.

These buildings were ideal homes for agricultural families. Daily activities mainly took place outside. The houses had roofs, but remained open at the sides, and the back room was used as a storage. Ladders or stairs were used to access additional space available on the roof, and upper rooms were also built. Since cooking and heating facilities were missing on the ground floor, the second story could serve as the living, sleeping and entertaining area. The ground floor was the economic domain used as storage for food and other items, and sometimes as a shelter for the family's livestock. Archaeological evidence shows that several houses were often joined together, thereby allowing larger extended families to live together and cooperate in their work.

Family as the basic unit of production: the role of cooperation

Family life was centred on and around agricultural production. As Joseph Blenkinsopp states: »As an economically independent unit, the typical household depended for its survival on possession of a plot of land for growing crops and access to grazing land for raising livestock, mostly sheep and goats. In identifying the typical household as an agrarian unit we should add that we know practically nothing about the urban family during the Israelite monarchy.«[13] Instead of describing the entire process of producing goods, I would like to emphasize the above-mentioned *cooperation*. Several working processes were infeasible for a sole nuclear family. Examples are fruit harvesting or reaping. This meant both shared work and a series of deals. Access to the number of tools necessary for production was often limited. When the harvest had been reaped, transportation became an important task. In addition, most village communities had only one threshing floor.[14] The necessity of cooperation confirms that on sociological and economic grounds, a clan equals a village or a restricted territory where people lived, worked, and amused themselves together.

[13] J. Blenkinsopp, The Family in First Temple Israel. In: L.G. Perdue and J. Blenkinsopp (eds.), Families in Ancient Israel, Louisville 1997, 53-54.

[14] For details see Oded Borowski, Agriculture in Iron Age Israel, Eisenbrauns, 2002; useful articles and informative photos: NEA 63/1-2 (2000).

Familial solidarity

In the social structure sketched above, familial solidarity was present on the social level of the clan. According to a widely accepted definition the clan is a protective association of families. In the ›pre-state period‹[15] there was no other force to guarantee acceptable behaviour. In monarchic times, the king's jurisdiction functioned like a court of appeal. Although we are not at all well informed about the legal praxis in Ancient Israel,[16] villages supposedly made decisions locally. In the monarchic period, the rich acted unjustly against the defenceless, and, in certain cases, the traditional solidarity could not solve personal damages. A very striking example is the case of the reaper whose garment was confiscated, as recorded on the Mesad Hasavyahu ostracon. »*May the Official, my lord, hear the plea of his servant. Your servant is working in the harvest ... Your servant did his reaping, finished, and stored (the grain) a few days ago before stopping (work). When your servant had finished (his) reaping ... Hoshayahu ben Shabay came and took your servant's garment ... All my companions will vouch for me, all who were reaping with me in the heat of the sun ... truly I am guiltless of any in[fraction]. [So please return] my garment ... You must not remain silent [when your servant is without garment].*« (Translation: Dennis Pardee)[17]

3 Family religion

Ancient Israelite religion was colourful. While reading the biblical texts it is tempting to look at the texts through the lens of the prophets and scribes: the Temple in the focus and strong monotheistic tendencies from the beginning. A more careful analysis of the texts changes the picture dramatically. Today, we talk about Israelite religions in plural,[18] and we distinguish between types of cultic life. Official religion was not at all that close to popular religion. For most Israelites, the

15 C. Meyers, The Family in Early Israel, 37. fn. 97.

16 J. Blenkinsopp, The Family in First Temple Israel, 59.

17 William W. Hallo, (ed.), The Context of Scripture. Vol. 3. Archival Documents from the Biblical World, Leiden 2002, 77-78.

18 See two recent monographs: Z. Zevit, The Religions of Ancient Israel. A Synthesis of Parallactic Approaches, London 2001; Richard S. Hess, Israelite Religions: An Archaeological and Biblical Survey, Grand Rapids 2007.

understanding of the divine world was closely paralleled by the neighbouring people. I am talking about the ordinary people from the villages of Judah; they most probably had religious convictions similar to Moabites or Edomites living under comparable circumstances. Generally speaking, we can distinguish between orthodox Yahwism, heterodox Yahwism, and syncretistic Yahwism.[19]

Orthodox Yahwism can be understood as the exclusive worship of YHWH, who was regarded as the sole effective divine power. Primary features were the lack of representation and sexual characteristics of God. Prophetic revelation and the casting of lots were acceptable ways of the utterance of the divine will, but other practices like necromancy were strictly prohibited. For centuries, local shrines were used, but by the end of Iron Age II the legitimate sacrifice was restricted to the Jerusalem temple. In sum, this was the kind of Yahwism the authors of the Hebrew Bible preferred.

»Heterodox Yahwism was an amalgam of the above.«[20] The most important differences between Orthodox and Heterodox practices and beliefs were the use of cult objects, divination, and veneration of the dead.

The term ›*syncretistic* Yahwism‹ seems to be odd at first glance. This term could be a misnomer but is intended to denote religious beliefs of those who followed both Baal and YHWH; those who bowed down before the sun, the moon and the hosts of heaven (Jer 8:1–3) also belonged to this category. The prophet Ezekiel clearly describes syncretistic practices in Jerusalem: »Then he brought me to the entrance of the house of the Lord; women were sitting there weeping for Tammuz. ... at the entrance of the house of the Lord, between the porch and the altar were about twenty-five men, with their backs to the temple of the Lord and their faces toward the east, prostrating themselves to the sun toward the east.« (Ez. 8, NRSV)

Family religion falls into the category of heterodox Yahwism. It should not be surprising that this was the most widespread form. The syncretistic views were held primarily by the educated elite, whereas orthodoxy was maintained by a concerned minority. The leader or at least the central figure of the family cult was the eldest living male

19 See the detailed description of these forms in P.D. Miller, The Religion of Ancient Israel, Louisville 2000, 47-62.

20 P.D. Miller, The Religion of Ancient Israel, 51.

member of the family.[21] The annual or periodically repeated feasts aside, the practices of circumcision, the observance of the Sabbath, and dietary regulations all took place within the family context. Central institutions such as the temple and the organized sacrificial system were unnecessary for these elements of religious life, which is why familial religious life continued undisturbed during the Babylonian exile. In the Iron Age, the cult in the Jerusalem Temple was not central in the life of most Israelite families: we should look at the First Temple as a royal chapel rather than a place of pilgrimage.

Probably the most important element of family religion was the veneration of the dead. These practices were connected to the land of the family. This land was not just a piece of soil for cultivation, but it also served as the burial site. Children had to honour their parents even in death, burying them with grateful respect, mourning (Jer 16:5), and setting up markers or monuments for them (2Sam 18:18; Gen 35:20). The interesting question would be what came next, but as orthodoxy opposed a cult of the dead, we do not know what was practised. Libations and food offerings were supposedly offered (as they were in the Mesopotamian *Kispu*, an important ritual of displacing hostile spirits and ensuring the prosperity of the family).[22] Archaeological excavations have found personal items, jewellery, tools, and pottery placed at the gravesites of the deceased; bowls are the most frequent form of pottery found in tombs.[23] A verse in Deuteronomy (26:14) can be seen as an indirect evidence of feeding the dead: »I have not eaten any of the sacred portions while I was in mourning, nor have I removed any of it while I was unclean, nor have I offered any of it to the dead. I have obeyed the LORD my God; I have done everything you commanded me.«[24] Besides these practices necromancy was also exercised – if not so, the condemnation of necromancers (Deut 18:11) would have been meaningless.

Most families used objects of ritual, like the well-known pillared figurines. These items were abominable in the sight of orthodox Yahwism, but for the majority accepting more heterodox views these figurines were parts of everyday piety. In households, dozens of offering stands have been found, while thus far forty or more limestone altars

21 R. Hess, Israelite Religions, 266-267.

22 J. Blenkinsopp, The Family in First Temple Israel, 81; E. Bloch-Smith, Judahite Burial Practices and Beliefs About the Dead, Sheffield 1991. 124.

23 E. Bloch-Smith, Judahite Burial Practices and Beliefs About the Dead, 72.

24 See also Ps 106:28; (Ps 16:4 is a possible reference to libations for the dead.)

have surfaced. The total number of figurines (female, equine, horse-and-rider, other anthropomorphic or zoomorphic vessels, etc.) equals a few thousand. I have to emphasize that findings in Palestine and Transjordan are homogeneous. During the 1999 and 2001 digging seasons archaeologists found an Iron Age Moabite site in Khirbet el-Mudayna, Jordan. Two monumental altars and an inscribed incense stand from a small sanctuary were dug up, neighbouring houses contributing small female figurines, a »hand-size« altar with decoration, and an equine figurine. The large number of female figurines that have been discovered must be emphasized: to date, 2000 or more have been unearthed.[25] These figures show a woman's torso; the upper body with the sometimes oversized breasts is always well-shaped, but the lower body is not shown. Most of these figurines are moulded, another sign of their popularity. What was their purpose? According to the majority of scholars they are either depictions of the mother goddess as a nursing mother, or representations of »a concept of the female deity principally as Mother and patroness of mothers.«[26] It is not the purpose of this paper to solve or even review the debate which was conducted during the past two decades over the veneration of Asherah in Ancient Israel, but I state most definitely that family religion included a female dimension too, a dimension which was underrepresented in the official cult.

4 *Conclusions*

One of the most intriguing questions of the biblical and theological perception of today's societies lies in the usage of parallels. Today's dominant social custom is the nuclear family and the single household. Neither of these was quite that important in the Ancient Near Eastern societies. How can we use biblical parallels in our reasoning concerning this particular issue? As a conclusion let me emphasize and bring under consideration three points:

25 W.G. Dever, What Did the Biblical Writers Know and When did they Know It? What Archaeology Can Tell Us about the Reality of Ancient Israel. Grand Rapids 2001, 193.

26 W.G. Dever, What Did the Biblical Writers Know and When did they Know It?, 150, 193.

1. The transformation into a monarchy did not cause a major disturbance in the social network of Ancient Israel. The main argument is that society remained agricultural in nature, methods of farming staying mostly the same. As a result, the everyday life of the families remained intact: we do not know about new phenomena such as large-scale slavery.
2. Family religion belonged to the heterodox understanding of Yahwism, with special emphasis on deceased ancestors and the feminine aspects. Family religion today is also full of hidden habits and ancient customs – the question is how the church should evaluate this clearly »unorthodox« issue.
3. Looking for the most prominent difference between today's western societies and their ancient parallels, we point to the existence and prominence of extended families and clans in the social structure. These groups had common economic ground and were central in practising familial solidarity.

In the 21st century these are important points, at least in Hungary, where I live and work. During the last few decades the traditional model of the family fell apart. Inside the church this is frequently interpreted using simple political and economic reasoning. While most people lived in the countryside, local family units survived. As household farming has lost its dominance in our societies, family sizes and populations diminish and sharp social tensions arise in affected villages. In accordance with the main points of this paper we emphasize the role of cooperation and family solidarity. In order to keep the agricultural village alive as a living part of our heritage we have to support local families. This is not just an economic debate, but also a question of biblical theology: although the notion of family changed during the last three millennia the keywords mentioned and emphasized above still characterize Christian families.

Jakobs Kampf mit sich selbst im Lichte der Gottesbegegnung

Eine tiefenpsychologische Auslegung[1]

Andrea Pethő-Udvardi

1 Einleitung, Fragestellungen

Immer wieder gerät die Gestalt des biblischen Jakob in den Fokus wissenschaftlicher Untersuchungen. Das Interesse an Jakob ist dabei nicht nur ein theologisches, sondern kann daneben auch andere Bereiche berühren. Die Person Jakobs wird im Folgenden nicht als historische Figur verstanden, sondern, methodisch stärker von literaturwissenschaftlichen Ansätzen her bestimmt, als eine paradigmatische Größe. Als solche kann sie auf unterschiedlichen Ebenen zum Paradigma werden – sei es kollektiv für das Handeln Gottes an Israel, sei es individuell, der Reflexion des eigenen Verhaltens und Gottesverhältnisses dienend. Im Rahmen der Erzählungen lädt sie so als Protagonist auf mehrfache Weise zur Identifikation ein. Aus dem breitgefächerten Spektrum möglicher Annäherungen heraus erfolgt nun in dieser Untersuchung insbesondere eine tiefenpsychologische Annäherung an Jakob.

Jakob ist eine komplexe Gestalt. Gerade seine Vielschichtigkeit, seine manchmal sogar gegensätzlichen Eigenschaften machen ihn zur perfekten Identifikationsfigur. Jede Leserin, jeder Leser kann einen

[1] Wegen der Konzentration auf die tiefenpsychologische Annäherung erfolgt die Auseinandersetzung mit der Sekundärliteratur zu den Jakobserzählungen nur dort, wo sie für die eigene Fragestellung nötig ist.

Punkt in der Gestalt oder in den Geschichten Jakobs finden, mit dem sie bzw. er sich identifizieren kann, einen Punkt, der es ermöglicht, in Jakobs Haut zu kriechen und sich so in ihm wieder zu finden.[2]

Die Geschichte von Jakob im Buch Genesis ist eine umfangreiche. Sie ergibt fast so wie eine Biographie, mit der Empfängnis beginnend bis zum Tod nach einem langen bewegten Leben. Doch sowohl in klassisch exegetischer als auch in archetypischer Sicht sind die Einzelstücke nicht aus biographischem Interesse zusammengefügt worden. Es wird in Wirklichkeit kein kontinuierlicher Lebenslauf erzählt, sondern es werden Schlaglichter auf existentiell und theologisch bedeutungsvolle Lebenssituationen geworfen. Versteht man die Geschichte Jakobs als seinen Entwicklungsprozess, kann der Kampf am Jabbok als sein Höhepunkt bezeichnet werden. Einzelstücke der Jakobsgeschichte, die mit den historisch-kritischen Methoden nur schwer zu erhellen sind, werden im Lichte des Ereignisses am Jabbok gelesen ganz neu verstehbar.

Im – in historisch-kritischer Perspektive – sogenannten Jakob-Esau-Sagenkranz finden wir, archetypisch betrachtet, das Leitmotiv für die Charakterisierung der Jakobgestalt insgesamt. Die Tiefenpsychologie unterscheidet dabei zwei Ebenen: die Objektstufe und die Subjektstufe.[3] Auf der Objektstufe zeigt sich dieses Motiv als der Kampf der feindlichen Brüder und ihre schließiche Versöhnung; auf der Subjektstufe finden wir das Motiv in der Doppelnatur von Jakobs Charakter: die helle und dunkle Seite in ihm.[4]

Im Folgenden wird versucht, sich der Jakobsgeschichte unter Fragen zu nähern wie: Wie ist die Familiendynamik bestimmt, in der Jakob aufgewachsen ist und die seinen Charakter, seine psychische Struktur prägt? Welche Wirkung haben die Familienbindungen, die Beziehungskräfte der Familieauf denIndividuationsprozess Jakobs? Wie kann die Integrität der Person (Jakob) durch die Familiendynamik gefördert oder gehindert werden?[5] Im Zusammenhang damit steht die Verknüpfung des Individuationsprozesses Jakobs und seiner Gottesbe-

2 Vgl. Renate Klein, Jakob, Wie Gott auf krummen Linien gerade schreibt, Leipzig 2007, 9-10.

3 Dazu genauer unter Punkt 2.

4 Vgl. Maria Kassel, Biblische Urbilder, Tiefenpsychologische Auslegung nach C. G. Jung, München 1980, 259.

5 Diese Fragestellungen werden auf der Ebene des plots der Erzählung verhandelt, ohne dabei etwas über eine mögliche Historizität der Jakobfigur zu sagen.

ziehung im Mittelpunkt meines Interesses, wofür der Kampf am Jabbok eine besondere Bedeutung hat.

Bevor auf die Jakobgestalt genauer eingegangen wird, werden zunächst zur methodischen Klärung noch einige grundlegende Bemerkungen zur tiefenpsychologischen Annäherung an die Texte gemacht.

2 *Tiefenpsychologische Bibelauslegung*

Die tiefenpsychologische Interpretation von biblischen Texten ist fast so alt wie die Tiefenpsychologie selbst.[6] Nach der anfänglich negativen Resonanz erlangte in den achtziger Jahren des 20. Jahrhunderts die Arbeit von Gerd Theissen und Eugen Drewermann[7] große Bedeutung für die Entwicklung einer immer reflektierter erfolgenden tiefenpsychologischen Interpretation des Neuen Testaments,[8] die dann auch für die Interpretation des Alten Testaments wichtig wurde.

Maria Kassel, eine der wichtigsten Vertreterinnen der tiefenpsychologischen Auslegung, betont, dass die meisten überlieferten Texte des Alten und Neuen Testaments nicht nur theologische Aussagen transportieren, sondern dass sie in einer Tiefenschicht menschliche Grunderfahrungen in religiöser Perspektive abgelagert haben, die von den Autoren und Tradenten oft gar nicht bewusst formuliert worden sind.[9]

Im Blick auf die bleibende Geltung überlieferter historischer Texte unterstreicht Drewermann: »die einzelne Begebenheit, die einzelne Szene muss in sich selbst als Typos von etwas allgemein Menschlichem verstanden werden und gleichzeitig muss vorausgesetzt werden, dass es im Menschen nicht nur ein Wesen an sich, sondern bestimmte Typen des Denkens, Vorstellens und Fühlens gibt, die zu allen Zeiten und Zonen einander gleich sind«[10].

6 Von S. Freud kann »Totem und Tabu« (1912) und »Der Mann Moses und die monotheistische Religion« (1939), von C. G. Jung »Antwort auf Hiob« (1952) erwähnt werden.

7 Drewermanns wichtigste Werke zum Thema Tiefenpsychologische Auslegung sind »Strukturen des Bösen«, Band I-III; »Tiefenpsychologie und Exegese« Band I-II, bei Theissen ist zu verweisen auf »Psychologische Aspekte paulinischer Theologie«, Paderborn.

8 Vgl. Wilhelm Pratscher, Tiefenpsychologie und Textauslegung, In: Siegfried Kreuzer, Dieter Vieweger, Proseminar I. Altes Testament, Stuttgart 2005, 199.

9 Vgl. Maria Kassel, Biblische Urbilder, 56.

10 Eugen Drewermann, Tiefenpsychologie und Exegese, Band I. Traum, Mythos, Märchen, Sage und Legende, Olten 1991, 375.

Die meisten Vertreter der tiefenpsychologischen Auslegung gehen davon aus, dass die wesentlichen Gedanken und Verfahren für eine solche Auslegung der biblischen Überlieferung im Denken des Psychologen Carl Gustav Jung zu finden sind. Gemeinsam mit Sigmund Freud vertritt Jung die Lehre von der Existenz zweier Bereiche in der menschlichen Psyche: das Bewusste und das Unbewusste. Nach Jung beruht das kollektive Unbewusste »auf einer tieferen Schicht, welche nicht mehr persönlicher Erfahrung und Erwerbung entstammt, sondern angeboren ist... Ich habe den Ausdruck ›kollektiv‹ gewählt, weil dieses Unbewusste nicht individueller, sondern allgemeiner Natur ist, das heißt, es hat im Gegensatz zur persönlichen Psyche Inhalte und Verhaltensweisen, welche überall und in allen Individuen die gleichen sind«.[11] Jung verwendet den Begriff »Archetypus«[12], um die von ihm angenommene, allen Menschen gemeinsame Bereitschaft und Fähigkeit zu bezeichnen, Faktoren und Motive, welche psychische Elemente sind, zu gewissen Bildern anzuordnen, und zwar in einer Art und Weise, die immer erst aus dem Effekt erkannt werden kann.[13]

Die tiefenpsychologische Auslegung geht davon aus, dass biblische Texte eine Oberflächen- und eine Tiefenstruktur aufweisen. Die Oberflächenstruktur (Objektstufe) wird durch die theologischen Aussagen bestimmt, die die Autoren bewusst formuliert haben; darauf richtet sich die Aufmerksamkeit der herkömmlichen Exegese. Die Tiefenstruktur (Subjektstufe) umfasst grundlegende menschliche Erfahrungen bzw. typische menschliche Lebensprozesse, die einen mehrdimensionalen Austausch zwischen Leser und Bibel ermöglichen.[14] Eine Auslegung, die sich darauf konzentriert, die Tiefenstruktur eines Textes zu verstehen, entlastet damit gleichzeitig das heutige Verständnis der Überlieferung vom Ballast vergangener Weltbilder.[15]

[11] Carl Gustav Jung, Erinnerungen, Träume, Gedanken, Zürich 1967, 418.

[12] Die wichtigsten Archetypen, die in tiefenpsychologischer Auslegung regelmässig begegnen, sind die Mutter, der Schatten, die feindlichen Brüder, der alte Weise, der Held, das göttliche Kind. Oft mit dem persönlichen Unbewussten gleichgesetzt, beinhaltet der Schatten den inferioren Teil der Persönlichkeit, das im bisherigen Leben Verdrängte oder die Noch-nicht-Persönlichkeit, deren Integration für die Individuation unumgänglich sei. Vgl. Anton A. Bucher, Bibel-Psychologie, Psychologische Zugänge zu biblischen Texten, Stuttgart 1992, 49.

[13] Vgl. Carl Gustav Jung, Der Mensch und seine Symbole, Olten 1979, 67.

[14] Vgl. Maria Kassel, Tiefenpsychologische Bibelauslegung, In: W. Langer, (Hrsg.) Handbuch der Bibelarbeit, München 1987, 157.

[15] Vgl. Horst Klaus Berg, Ein Wort wie Feuer, Wege lebendiger Bibelauslegung, München 1991, 146.

Das Bestreben der tiefenpsychologischen Auslegung wird von Maria Kassel prägnant formuliert: »Die tiefenpsychologische Auslegung der Bibel ist eine noch ungewohnte, aber vielversprechende Möglichkeit, das Stadium des nur rationalen und kritischen Umgangs mit der Bibel zu überschreiten und überlieferte Zeugnisse gelebten Glaubens in unser Leben hereinzuholen.«[16]

3 Die Möglichkeiten der Entwicklung der Personalität

Die Grundcharakterisierung der Jakobgestalt

Die Entwicklung der Person Jakobs bzw. seiner Persönlichkeit ist bestimmt von den Familienbeziehungen und der Familiendynamik, in denen er aufwuchs.[17] Als Erwachsener führt er die Muster, die er innerhalb der Familie gelernt hat, mit ihren Lösungsmechanismen weiter. Diese geben nicht nur über ihn selbst, sondern auch über die Verhaltensstrategien seiner Eltern Auskunft. Diese Muster gibt Jakob dann ebenso weiter und zeigt sie beispielhaft seinen Kindern. So sind die sich in den verschiedenen Generationen wiederholende Rivalität, das Hintergehen, der Betrug, die Gewalt nicht zufällig. Die Kinder erben sie quasi auf der Basis des Verhaltens der Eltern. Aber auch wenn die angelernten Muster Menschen bestimmen, verurteilt das Verhalten der Eltern nicht automatisch zu deren Wiederholung. Die Möglichkeit zur Veränderung und Entwicklung, zum Einbringen neuer Verhaltensweisen ist gegeben, wie das Beispiel Jakobs zeigt: Helmut Hark hat in seiner Arbeit zum Traum auf wesentliche Punkte aufmerksam gemacht, die für die weitere Untersuchung von Belang sind: »Das geistig-psychische Familienerbe und die biologische Erbmasse sind nicht die einzigen Exponenten für die Entwicklung einer Person. Hinzu kommen die persönlichen Erfahrungen, vor allem die unzähligen Anpassungen und Ausstoßungen im Leben. Zu dem Erbe und der Anpassung kommt schließlich die ganz persönliche Eigenart. Diese Originalität, die Besonderheit seiner eigenen Existenz zu erkennen und zu verwirk-

16 Maria Kassel, Sei, der du werden sollst, Tiefenpsychologische Impulse aus der Bibel, München 1982, 2.

17 Hier ist erneut daran zu erinnern, dass es um den Protagonisten einer Erzählung, nicht um eine historische Gestalt geht.

lichen, ist die eigentliche Aufgabe des Jakob und eines jeden Menschen.«[18]

In der Familie Jakobs herrschte eine ganz bestimmte Familiendynamik. Buchstäblich vom Mutterleibe an musste sich Jakob mit seinem Bruder »herumschlagen« und auseinandersetzen. Aber nicht nur die Beziehung zwischen den Brüdern, sondern auch die zu den Eltern wird von Gegensätzen bestimmt: Während Esau vom Vater bevorzugt wird, ist Jakob der geliebte Sohn der Mutter.

Jakob ist die einzige Figur unter den Erzeltern, die vom Mutterleib an bis zum Begräbnis die wesentlichen Stationen eines Menschenlebens bietet.[19] So enthält die Geschichte Jakobs typische, dem jeweiligen Alter entsprechende Lebensthemen: die Bindung an ein Elternteil, die Kämpfe mit den Geschwistern, die Suche nach einem Lebenspartner, die Zeugung von Kindern, das Ringen um einen geachteten Stand im Beruf und in der Familie, die Konflikte der Polygamie, die unterschiedliche Beziehung zu den Kindern und die Weitergabe von Verhaltensmustern in der Familie.[20]

Die Gestalt Jakobs ist durchgehend charakterisiert durch das Dominieren des Verstandes sowie die stark ausgebildete Fähigkeit, auch durchzusetzen, was er für sich als richtig und gut erkennt. Fast scheint es, als seien ihm diese Fähigkeiten angeboren, denn schon bei der Geburt wird er als einer gezeichnet, der seine eigene Situation verbessern und vornedran sein will. Da auf der Subjektebene Esau die andere Seite Jakobs ist, stellt Jakobs Festhalten der Ferse Esaus bei der Geburt (Gen 25,26) aber nicht ein biographisches Detail dar, sondern einen Wesenszug Jakobs, der in den weiteren Geschichten verschärfte Umrisse erhält. Jakob setzt alles daran, der Erste zu sein: Er gewinnt das Erstgeburtsrecht, er betrügt seinen Vater, um den Segen zu erhalten.

4 Die Beziehungen Jakobs

Die Beziehungen innerhalb der Familie spielen sich auf unterschiedlichen Ebenen ab. Da ist zum einen die Beziehung der Eltern

[18] Helmut Hark, Der Traum als Gottes vergessene Sprache, Symbolpsychologische Deutung biblischer und heutiger Träume, Olten 1985, 36.

[19] Vgl. Anneliese Hecht, Lebensweg als Glaubensweg, Die Themen und Leitwörter der Jakobserzählung, In: Bettina Wellmann, (Hrsg.) Die Jakobserzählung – Rivalen und Gesegnete, Stuttgart, 2009 10.

[20] Vgl. Anneliese Hecht, Lebensweg als Glaubensweg, 11.

untereinander. Zum anderen spielt die Beziehung zwischen Eltern und Kindern eine wesentliche Rolle, bei der noch einmal zu differenzieren ist zwischen dem Vater und den Söhnen sowieso der Mutter und ihren Söhnen. Dabei spielt sich die eigentliche Beziehung zwischen Rebekka und Jakob ab. Schließlich ist die das Geschehen dominierende Beziehung zwischen den beiden Brüdern in den Blick zu nehmen.

4.1 Die Eltern

4.1.1 Das Verhältnis zwischen Isaak[21] und Rebekka[22]

Über die Gestalt Isaaks wissen wir wenig. In Gen 25 kommt Isaak im Alter von vierzig Jahren zu seiner Ehefrau Rebekka, die aus der Sippe des Vaterbruders Nahor stammt.[23] Die Zahl 40 ist wohl eher als eine symbolische zu verstehen angesichts dessen, dass diese Zahl im Alten Testament mit Vorliebe verwendet wird, wo es um Krisensituationen oder einschneidende Veränderungen geht.[24] Zum Zeitpunkt der Brautwerbung stellt der Text Rebekka als ein Mädchen von sehr schöner Gestalt dar, als eine Jungfrau, die noch keinen Mann erkannt hatte. Isaak und Rebekka, wie später auch Jakob und Rachel, trafen sich bei einem Brunnen, was an einen numinosen Ort denken lässt, an dem sowohl Gotteserfahrungen als auch Trost möglich sind.[25] In der Erzählung von der Brautwerbung Gen 24 erweist sich Rebekka als entschlossene junge Frau, die bereit ist, sich auf das Unbekannte einzulassen und somit den Willen Gottes zu erfüllen.

Die Notiz, dass Isaak sich mit Rebekka über den Verlust seiner Mutter Sara hinwegtröstete (Gen 24,66f), lässt auf eine enge Mutter-Sohn-Beziehung zwischen Isaak und Sara rückschließen. Das Muster wiederholt sich, denn auch im Leben Rebekkas wird die wichtigste Beziehung nicht die zu ihrem Ehemann, sondern die zu ihrem Sohn Jakob sein.[26]

21 Vgl. http://www.bibelwissenschaft.de/wibilex/das-bibel-lexikon/details/quelle/WIBI/referenz/21862/

22 Vgl. http://www.bibelwissenschaft.de/wibilex/das-bibel-lexikon/details/quelle/WIBI/referenz/32823/

23 Nach Gen 24,15 eine Enkelin Nahors.

24 So u.a. die 40-jährige Wüstenwanderung, Moses 40-tägiger Aufenthalt am Sinai, Elias 40-tägige Wanderung zum Horeb.

25 Vgl. Helmut Hark, Der Traum als Gottes vergessene Sprache, 58.

26 Vgl. Helmut Hark, Der Traum als Gottes vergessene Sprache, 58.

Rebekka leidet zwanzig Jahre lang unter ihrer Unfruchtbarkeit, bis sie schwanger wird und ein göttliches Orakel (Gen 25,23) ihre Schwangerschaftsbeschwerden mit dem Hinweis auf eine anstehende Zwillingsgeburt deutet. Die Aussage dieses Orakels lässt ferner den Konflikt zwischen den noch nicht geborenen Brüdern erahnen und kann als programmatisch für die gesamte Jakobsgeschichte angesehen werden. Nicht minder deutlich für die Darstellung des Konflikts zwischen den Zwillingsbrüdern Jakob und Esau ist die Vorliebe je eines Elternteils für jeweils einen ihrer Söhne: »Und Isaak hatte Esau lieb und aß gern von seinem Wildbret; Rebekka aber hatte Jakob lieb.« (Gen 25,28). Esau als Liebling des Vaters wird als ein Jäger ohne tiefere geistige Bedürfnisse, als behaart und stark gezeichnet. Jakob, der Muttersohn, wird dargestellt als ein sanfter Mann, in Zelten wohnend, zu Träumen und zu Tränen neigend.[27] Diese Attribute werden jedoch nirgends als Begründung für die jeweilige Bevorzugung durch ein Elternteil genannt. Diese bleibt in ihrer Begründung vielmehr offen.[28]

4.1.2 Isaak und seine Söhne: Esau und Jakob

Für Isaak ist die eine bedeutungsvolle Szene in seiner Beziehung zu den Söhnen die Weitergabe des Segens. Auf der Objektstufe kann die Geschichte als der Versuch Jakobs verstanden werden, sich die fehlende Bestätigung durch den Vater zu erzwingen und dessen Konzentration auf Esau zu durchbrechen, nachdem Jakob vergeblich die fehlende väterliche Anerkennung gesucht hat. Auf der Subjektstufe stellt sich die Erschleichung des Segens als der Versuch dar, Ganzheit und Fülle des Lebens mit Hilfe einer List auf bequeme Weise zu erlangen, statt durch einen intensiven Wandlungsprozess mit ihr eins zu werden.[29] Der Segen ist hier, wie auch in anderen Stellen im Alten Testament, ein Integrationssymbol,[30] das archetypisch Fruchtbarkeit und Ganzheit der menschlichen Existenz anzeigt.

[27] Vgl. Dorothee Sölle, Gottes starke Töchter, Grosse Frauen der Bibel, Ostfildern 2003, 30.

[28] Vgl. Lawrence Richards, Alle Frauen der Bibel, Giessen 2003, 58. Darin trifft sich die Erzählung mit der grund-losen Erwählung Israels durch JHWH, die allenfalls eine Begründung in Dtn 7,7f. findet im Hinweis auf JHWHs Liebe.

[29] Vgl. Maria Kassel, Biblische Urbilder, 260-261.

[30] Der Begriff »Integration« bezeichnet in der Psychologie den Prozess, der die verschiedenen Erfahrungen, Triebe, Fertigkeiten, Wahrnehmungen zu einem Ganzen zusammenführt. Die geglückte Integration der Erlebnis- und der Verhaltensfunktionen wird zum Maßstab eines gesunden Seelenlebens. So mit Art. Integration, Leszczynski, Christian, Schuhmann, Wilfried (Hrsg.), Lexikon

Eine besondere Spannung kann die Auslegung der Jakobserzählungen erhalten, wenn wir in Rechnung stellen, dass aus tiefenpsychologischer Sicht die Menschengruppen, die in Isaaks Segen genannt werden, die reich differenzierten Möglichkeiten von Jakobs psychischen Teilkräften benennen können. Das Bewusstmachen dieser Teilkräfte bzw. ihr Heraufholen aus dem Unbewussten sowie die daraus folgende Zuordnung zum Bewusstseinszentrum ermöglichen das Schaffen einer Ganzheit des Selbst, was das eigentliche Ziel auch des Lebens Jakobs ist.[31]

Esau hat eine besondere Nähe zum Vater, der die Ahnenreihe und damit das Alte, seit langem Vorhandene repräsentiert. Maria Kassel macht darauf aufmerksam, dass Esaus Erstgeburtsrecht zum Ausdruck der Vorherrschaft unbewusster Mächte in der Menschheitsentwicklung wird, in deren Verlauf das individuelle Bewusstsein, noch mehr die logisch-kritische Ratio, eine spätere Errungenschaft ist.[32] Das Faktum, dass Esau sich fremde Frauen nimmt (Gen 26,34f.), was besonders Rebekka schaudern macht (Gen 27,46), zeigt die Fremdheit und Ferne dieser tiefen Schicht des Unbewussten gegenüber dem Bewusstsein.

4.1.3 Rebekka und Jakob

Die Jakobserzählungen berichten über die ausgeprägte besondere Beziehung zwischen der Mutter und ihrem jüngeren Sohn. Rebekka spielt eine wichtige Rolle beim Erlangen des Segens durch Jakob. Ja, sie hat eine dominierende, gar befehlende Kraft im Leben ihres Sohnes, der Jakob nicht ausweichen kann.

Rebekka ist diejenige, die Jakob zum Betrug am Vater anstiftet (Gen 27). Hier spielt der Archetyp der Anima eine wichtige Rolle: Der Betrug ist in archetypischer Aussage ein Selbstbetrug, und Jakob wird durch Rebekka zur Anima-Figur. Die Idee der Täuschung stammt von ihr, sie heckt die Einzelheiten des Täuschungsmanövers aus (Gen 27,5–10). Von der Anima-Seite rührt Jakobs schlaue Erfindungsgabe her. Sie ist der Motor zur Ausbildung seiner intellektuellen Einseitigkeit. Sie schneidet auch sein Bewusstsein von seiner unbewussten Lebensquelle ab. Indem Rebekka Jakob zur Flucht vor Esau verleitet (Gen 27,42–46), verstärkt

der Psychologie, Wissen Media Verlag, Gütersloh 1995, 201. Vgl. u.a. die Abraham- und die Exodusüberlieferung.

31 Vgl. Maria Kassel, Biblische Urbilder, 260.

32 Maria Kassel, Biblische Urbilder, 265. Sie bietet leider keine genaueren Hinweise auf die Basis für diese Überlegungen; da sie aber in ihrer Konsequenz in den Duktus meiner Textauslegung passen, scheinen sie mir plausibel.

sie seine Anima-Seite. Jakob ist damit als ein Mann gezeichnet, der dem Einfluss einer unintegrierten Anima erliegt. Diese Anima verhindert seine menschliche Entwicklung, denn er bleibt von seiner dunklen, aber schöpferischen Seite (von Esau) getrennt. Jakob folgt dem von Rebekka ausgewählten Reiseziel mit der Flucht zu ihrem Bruder Laban. Das heißt aber, dass Jakob auf diesem seinem Weg dem Bannkreis der unintegrierten Anima nicht entkommen und ein unreifer Mensch bleiben wird.[33]

4.2. Die Auseinandersetzung mit Esau[34]

Charakteristikum der meisten Brüderpaartraditionen[35] ist das wechselseitige Bestimmungs-verhältnis, in dem die Brüder zueinander stehen. Jeder der Brüder ist, was er ist, nur im Verhältnis zum anderen.[36] Esau ist eine unverkennbare Personalisierung der anderen Seite Jakobs. Er ist als Gegentyp zu dem hellen, ordentlichen, sein Leben planenden Jakob gezeichnet. Sein Verhalten ist von Trieb bestimmt, er hat den »primitiveren«, den archaischen Beruf des Jägers, im Gegensatz zu Jakobs Beruf des Hirten. Die konfliktreiche Beziehung zu seinem Bruder Jakob steht in den Jakob-Esau-Erzählungen deutlich im Vordergrund. Als der Schatten Jakobs verkörpert Esau die animalische und ungesteuerte Triebhaft in ihm, eine Urkraft, die sich umsetzt in unkontrolliertes Tun.

Erzählungen vom Kampf des Menschen mit seinem abgewehrten, aber doch mitleben wollenden Schatten kommen in der Bibel häufig vor.[37] Der Selbstwerdungsprozess, der nötig ist zur Integration des Schattens, lässt sich beschreiben als der Kampf zwischen den beiden Prinzipien Schatten und Bewusstsein, bei dem Fortschritte erzielt

33 Vgl. Maria Kassel, Biblische Urbilder, 262.

34 Vgl. http://www.bibelwissenschaft.de/wibilex/das-bibellexikon/details/quelle/WIBI/referenz/17748/

35 Die wichtigsten sind: Kain und Abel, Jakob und Esau, Moses und Aron. Im Alten Testament spielen Schwesternpaare keine Rolle, doch ein Blick auf die Erzählung von Marta und Maria im Neuen Testament (Lukas 10,38-42) zeigt, dass für das hier verhandelte Problem das Geschlecht allenfalls auf der Objektebene in Rolle spielt, nicht aber auf der Subjektebene.

36 Vgl. Johanna Erzberger, Brüderpaare In.: Gerhard Langer (Hrsg.), Esau – Bruder und Feind, Göttingen 2009, 117.

37 Das wichtigste Beispiel ist Gen 4, aber im Neuen Testament können auch Schattenprobleme, z.B. in Lukas 15, in der Geschichte des verlorenen Sohnes und in Lukas 10, in der Geschichte von Maria und Marta, wahrgenommen werden.

werden durch errungene Teileinigungen der beiden psychischen Seiten auf einer jeweils höheren Ebene des Bewusstseins. Der Kampf mit dem Schatten bildet die bleibende Basis für die psychische Entwicklung des Menschen. In der Bibel ist die Auseinandersetzung mit dem Schatten meistens auch der Anfang für neue Gotteserfahrung.[38] Ein schattenloses Dasein, also eines, bei dem der Mensch so lebt, als habe er keinen Schatten, eines, in dem er sich seinen Schatten nicht bewußt macht, schneidet nach biblischem Verständnis den Menschen von seiner transzendenten Dimension ab.[39] So hat die Schattenproblematik aus sich heraus einen religiösen Aspekt.

Das erste Bruderpaar in der Bibel veranschaulicht eine starke Gefährlichkeit des menschlichen Schattenproblems, sowohl auf der Objekt-, als auch auf der Subjektebene. Die Objektebene, identisch mit der Weltgeschichte, zeigt Brudermord als Vernichtung des Mitmenschen. Auf der Subjektebene kann das Stadium der menschlichen Bewusstseinsentwicklung beobachtet werden, in dem das Ich als psychische Bewusstseinsinstanz mit der Erkenntnis und Steuerungsfunktion für den gesamten psychischen Organismus aus dem psychischen Ozean des Unbewussten auftaucht, das Stadium, in dem der Mensch beginnt, sich als Individuum zu fühlen, und lernen muss, als einzelner Verantwortung für sein Tun und Lassen zu übernehmen.[40]

Erst durch die Integration des Schattens wird sich die Urgewalt des Unbewussten nicht mehr zerstörend, sondern schöpferisch auswirken.[41] Solange Jakob die Komplexität seiner Psyche und ihrer Antriebskräfte leugnet, indem er sie in die Eindimensionalität der rationalen Kräfte zwingen will, ist sein Schatten ihm gefährlich. Dies wird in der Morddrohung Esaus gegen Jakob symbolisiert.

4.3. Die Beziehungen in der späteren Familie

4.3.1 Der Konflikt mit Laban

Als Onkel Jakobs ist Laban noch der Retter, derjenige, der Herberge anbietet. Als Schwiegervater aber wird er zum Rivalen. Mit dem Betrug in der Brautnacht gibt er ohne Zweifel Jakob zurück, was dieser an

38 Vgl. die vorherige Anmerkung.

39 Vgl. Maria Kassel, Sei, der du werden sollst, Tiefenpsychologische Impulse aus der Bibel, München 1982, 12.

40 Vgl. Maria Kassel, Sei, der du werden sollst, 37.

41 Vgl. Maria Kassel, Biblische Urbilder, 264.

seinem Bruder und an seinem Vater verschuldete.[42] In Laban begegnet Jakob seinem Spiegelbild. In dem Betrüger Laban kann sich Jakob selbst betrachten und so an seiner Reifung arbeiten.[43] Aus tiefenpsychologischer Sinn wird Jakobs Rivalität mit Laban in der religiösen Dimension menschheitlicher Erfahrung interpretiert. In archetypischer Sicht bedeutet das eine Konfrontation Jakobs mit sich selbst; Jakob kann sich erst dann wirklich betrachten, wenn er sich selbst, seinen eigenen dunklen Seiten, seiner eigenen Schuldhaftigkeit gegenüber steht und sich mit sich selbst versöhnt.[44] Diese Einheit mit sich selbst wird dann auch zur Begegnung mit Gott. Die Begegnung mit Laban bietet Jakob die Möglichkeit, seinen Selbstbetrug zu erkennen und sein Leben zu ändern. Aber Jakob lernt aus der Selbstbegegnung nichts, er bleibt, wie er ist. Als ihm das eigene Spiegelbild unerträglich wird, verhält er sich ihm gegenüber wie gegenüber seiner Schattenseite, er ergreift die Flucht (Gen 31,20f).

Obwohl Jakob in den Taten Labans seinen eigenen Betrug erkannt hat und erlebt, welches Gefühl das Frustriertsein ist, so gibt es doch einen Unterschied zwischen den Taten und der Motivation der beiden Gestalten. Auf Jakob liegt trotz seiner Fehltritte der Segen Gottes , was wir daran sehen, wie Gott mit ihm im Traum bei Bethel vor seiner Reise nach Haran Kontakt aufnimmt. Obwohl Jakobs Betrug im Lichte seine Erwählung nicht verkleinert werden kann, kann aber der Lebensweg als ein Glaubensweg angeschaut werden, auf dem ein Mensch Gott in allen Lebensphasen und Lebenssituationen erfahren kann.

4.3.2 Jakob und seine kämpfenden Frauen

Schon die Einführung der beiden Schwestern Lea und Rahel[45] in Gen 29,16–18 enthält wichtige Informationen für den Konflikt, der sich zwischen ihnen anbahnt. Die jüngere Rahel ist schön, von der älteren Lea wird dies dagegen nicht gesagt. Dementsprechend gilt Jakobs Zuneigung Rahel, und er arbeitet für sie sieben Jahre bei seinem Onkel.

42 Auffallend ist, dass wiederum ein Gegeneinander von Jüngerem und Älterem im Hintergrund steht, was sich dann noch einmal wiederholt beim Geschwisterpaar Lea und Rahel.

43 Vgl. Renate Klein, Jakob, Wie Gott auf krummen Linien gerade schreibt, Leipzig 2007, 209.

44 Vgl. Maria Kassel, Biblische Urbilder, 262.

45 Vgl. http://www.bibelwissenschaft.de/wibilex/das-bibellexikon/details/quelle/WIBI/referenz/32450/

Es wird nur wenig über die Beziehung zwischen den beiden Schwestern gesagt, bevor sie Jakob heiraten, aber eine gewisse Rivalität ist bereits zu erahnen. Der Konflikt wird geschürt durch den Hochzeitsbetrug in Gen 29,22–27. Die Rivalität zwischen den Schwestern bricht dann voll aus in der Erzählung über die Geburt der Kinder Jakobs. Rahel steht – nach Sara und Rebekka – in der dritten Generation zunächst unfruchtbarer Frauen, muss dem Kinderglück ihrer Schwester Lea zusehen und sich lange mit der Leihmutterschaft begnügen.[46] Die von Jakob weniger geliebte Lea bringt vier Söhne zur Welt (Ruben, Simeon, Levi, Juda), während Rahel, deren Name mit der Bedeutung »Mutterschaf« verstanden werden kann, der Ironie des Schicksals unterliegt und zunächst unfruchtbar bleibt; dann hatte auch sie zwei Kinder (Josef und Benjamin). Die Beziehung zwischen den Schwestern nach der Heirat mit Jakob ist gekennzeichnet von Eifersucht, Rivalität und gegenseitigen Verletzungen.[47] Die in den Erzählungen dargestellten Konflikte spielen aber nicht nur in der Oberflächenstruktur eine Rolle, sondern sind auch auf einer tieferen Ebene zu verstehen. So formuliert Renate Klein nicht zufällig: »Die psychologische Auslegung transferiert die Konfliktgeschichten des Jakoberzählkreises von außen nach innen. Die Konflikte spielen sich im Inneren Jakobs ab. Selbst der Konflikt zwischen Rahel und Lea wird als innerer Zwiespalt Jakobs angesehen. Er schwankt zwischen der Frau als Mutter (Lea) und der Frau als Geliebter (Rahel). Es geht also um die Integrierung dieser zwiespältigen Gefühlswelt.«[48]

Die Rivalität zwischen den Frauen setzt sich unter den Kinder Jakobs fort. Der Vater verneint nicht, dass er die von der geliebten Frau geborenen Kinder mehr liebt als die der anderen. Er hebt Josef besonders hervor und stellt ihn an die erste Stelle. So laufen der Bruderzwist, die Lüge und der Betrug in der späteren Familie Jakobs weiter.

46 Vgl. Dorothee Sölle, Gottes starke Töchter, Grosse Frauen der Bibel, Ostfildern 2003, 35.

47 Vgl. Lawrence Richards, Alle Frauen der Bibel, Giessen 2003, 65.

48 Renate Klein, Jakob, Wie Gott auf krummen Linien gerade schreibt, 209.

5 Das Wachstum Jakobs, sein Individuationsprozess, seine Integrität

5.1. Die Integrität Jakobs

Die Integrität Jakobs kommt am deutlichsten in Gen 25,27 zur Sprache. In der Übersetzung von Gerhard von Rad finden wir den Vers wie folgt wiedergegeben: »Als nun die Knaben groß wurden, da ward Esau ein Mann, der sich auf die Jagd verstand, ein Mann, der sich auf dem Feld umhertrieb; Jakob aber ein ordentlicher Mann, der bei den Zelten blieb«.[49] Luther übersetzt demgegenüber: Jakob war ein gesitteter Mann, und nach Buber war Jakob ein schlichter Mann.

Wer war nun aber Jakob? Ein ordentlicher, ein gesitteter oder ein schlichter Mann? Das hebräische Wort תָּם bedeutet vor allem: fromm, rechtschaffen, reinlich. Zum Wortfeld gehört auch תֹּם mit der Bedeutung ganz, vollendet, fertig.

Das Adjektiv תָּם erscheint relativ häufig im Hiobbuch (7mal תָּם, 3mal תֲּמִם). Das Wort findet sich auch in Gen 17,2, wo Gott zu Abraham sagt: »wandle vor mir und sei fromm«.[50]

Die תָּם wie תֹּם zugrundeliegende hebräische Sprachwurzel תמם bedeutet: vollständig werden/sein. In der allgemeinen Umgangssprache hatte sie die Bedeutung: fertig werden/sein.[51] Unser Wort ist also nicht von einer christlichen oder moralischen Vorstellung von Vollkommenheit gefüllt, sondern kennzeichnet den Weg hin zur Vollkommenheit. In moderner Sprache können wir von der Integrität der Person sprechen. תמם ist nach Pedersen Integrität als Qualität der Seele. Aber es geht nicht nur um die Seele, sondern auch darum, dass der Rechtschaffene in Integrität handelt und sein Tun Integrität ist; dies drückt sich aus durch den Weg der Ganzwerdung. תמם kann auch das Resultat eines solchen Weges bezeichnen, nämlich Glücklichsein.[52]

5.2. Jakobs Wandlung im Ringen mit dem Unbekannten

Der Weg zur Integrität, zur Individuation, war für Jakob keineswegs geradlinig. Genesis 32 berichtet über seinen nächtlichen Kampf, der mit der Namengebung als symbolischer Wiedergeburt, als schmerzvoller

49 Gerhard von Rad, Das 1. Buch Mose. Genesis, ATD 2-4., Göttingen 1987, 211.

50 Vgl. Klaus Koch, Art. תמם, In.: THAT 2., München 1976, 1049.

51 Vgl. Kedar-Kopfstein, Art. תמם, In.: ThWAT, VIII., Stuttgart 1995, 691.

52 Vgl. Klaus Koch, Art. תמם, In.: THAT 2., München 1976, 1049.

Vervollständigung seiner selbst interpretiert werden kann. Jakob kehrt in seiner Lebensmitte nach einer langen Verbannung in seine Heimat zurück. Dies geschieht nicht allein; bei ihm sind seine Frauen, seine Kinder, seine Knechte und alles, was er im Laufe seines bisherigen Lebens erreicht hat. Unter psychologischem Aspekt kann daraus gelesen werden, dass er unterwegs, auf dem Weg nach Hause, seinen Taten, sich selbst, ins Auge sehen muss.

Die Ereignisse am Jabbok[53] brechen für Jakob eine Welt auf, die schon immer zu ihm gehörte, zu der ihm jedoch der Zugang verstellt war. Sein Schatten fällt mit der Urgewalt der archetypischen Bilder in seine abgeschirmte Ich-Sphäre ein und ermöglicht Jakob zum ersten Mal ein wirkliches Transzendieren seiner engen Ich-Welt. Indem er diese Transzendenz zur Nachtseite seines Selbst zulässt, erfährt er Gott.[54]

Der Flussübergang ist das Symbol[55] für eine Umbruchsituation im Leben des Menschen, er ist ein Archetyp der Wandlung. Der Fluss ist für Jakob die Grenze, die er nur als gewandelter Mensch oder gar nicht überschreiten kann. Psychisch gesehen, ermöglicht ihm die Wandlung das Überschreiten und damit das Leben, die Verweigerung der Wandlung aber wäre sein Tod.[56]

53 Das Ringen Jakobs mit dem איש) wird mit dem Verbum אבק) ausgedrückt (Er »rang mit ihm« wörtlich: »klammerte sich fest«). Scharbert, 1986, 221, vermutet, dass die Erzählung einmal mit dem Satz: »Deshalb nannte er den Fluss Jabbok« geendet haben muss, denn die Wahl des seltenen אבק) muss mit Jabbok zusammenhängen.

54 Vgl. Maria Kassel, Biblische Urbilder, 268.

55 Bucher 1992 bietet eine Auslegung von Gen 32,23–32, wobei er in Kapitel 1 auf die Auslegung von S. Freud eingeht, im 2. Kapitel auf die von C. G. Jung, die er mit einigen Beobachtungen von M. Kassel ergänzt. Während es sich im ersten Falle um einen ödipalen sexuellen Konflikt gehandelt habe, so im zweiten um eine schmerzhafte Konfrontation mit den dunklen Schichten des eigenen Selbst, die sich für die Individuation aber als förderlich erwiesen habe. Noch deutlicher treten die Unterschiede hervor, wenn die Interpretationen der einzelnen Motive einander gegenüber gestellt werden:
Das Motiv »Fluss« ist nach Freud das Symbol der eigenen Mutter, nach Jung/Kassel aber das archetypische Symbol der Wandlung. Das Motiv »Engel« ist nach Freud das Symbol des Phallus, nach Jung/Kassel das Symbol des eigenen Schattens. Das Motiv »die ausgerenkte Hüfte« bedeutet nach Freud die symbolische Kastration, nach Jung/Kassel die Folge der Anerkennung des Schattens. Nach Freud ist »Esau« das Symbol des Vaters, nach Jung/Kassel ist er Jakobs eigener Schatten. Vgl. Anton A. Bucher, Bibel-Psychologie, Psychologische Zugänge zu biblischen Texten, Stuttgart 1992, 42.

56 Ein verbreitetes Motiv ist der unbekannte, unbenennbare gefährliche Geist, der an einem Fluss lokalisiert ist und der nur bei Nacht über Menschen Macht hat.

Ausgelöst wird der Kampf durch die Rückkehr zu Esau, was zugleich die Reaktivierung der Schattenproblematik bedeutet. Es erfolgt eine Rückwendung ins Innere, die dadurch ermöglicht und herausgefordert wird, dass Jakob die Grenzen der Dominanz des Bewusstseins erreicht hat. Die Unterdrückung des Unterbewusstseins ist nicht länger möglich, Gefühle können nicht mehr mit Hilfe des Verstandes ausgeschaltet werden. Jakob konnte seinen bisherigen Lebensentwurf nicht mehr weiterführen. In Gen 32 wird erzählt, wie Jakob gestellt wird und sich unausweichlich mit der zurückgelassenen Seite seines Lebens befassen muss. Er wird zu einer Neustrukturierung seines Lebens gezwungen.[57]

Was sich am Jabbok ereignet, geschieht völlig überraschend und ist für den Betroffenen in höchstem Maße bedrohlich. Es vollzieht sich in der Nacht und in der Einsamkeit – beides ist für das Geschehen konstitutiv. Es gibt keinen Zeugen. Die nächsten Menschen sind von den beiden Kämpfenden durch den Fluss getrennt, [58] so dass keine Hilfe von außen erwartet werden kann. Auch wird damit deutlich gemacht, dass keine Ablenkung gegeben ist, die den entscheidenden Prozess behindern könnte.

In der Lage, in der Jakob sich selbst nicht mehr entkommen kann, überfällt ihn der anonyme Kampfpartner, der unbestimmt als איש), also »einer« oder »ein Mann« genannt wird. Die Anonymität kennzeichnet genau Jakobs bisherige Einstellung zu seinem Schatten: er wollte ihn nicht wahrhaben, deshalb kennt er ihn nicht.

Doch mit wem rang Jakob? Mit JHWH, mit dem Gott seines Vaters, mit einem Flussdämon[59]? In der exegetischen Fachliteratur finden sich

Der Flussgott als dämonische Macht versinnbildet das Gefährliche von Übergangs- oder Krisensituationen.

57 Vgl. Maria Kassel, Biblische Urbilder, 272.

58 Vgl. Hans Jochen Boecker, 1 Mose 25,12–37,1, Isaak und Jakob, ZBK 1,3, Zürich 1992, 101.

59 Jakob war ganz allein am Jabbok, der Kampf war ein Überfall und der Angreifer muss seine Identität verbergen - alle drei Züge passen zum feindlichen Dämon oder bösen Geist, wie er in vielen Religionen auf der ganzen Welt begegnet. Im Neuen Testament ist es besonders der eine Krankheit verursachende böse Geist, hier ist es ein Nacht- oder Flussdämon, die Verkörperung der Gefährlichkeit eines Flussüberganges. Diese im Animismus wurzelnde Vorstellung ist verbreitet und in den drei genannten Zügen so präzise beschrieben, dass man dem nicht ausweichen kann: Der Text spricht von einem feindlichem Dämon oder bösen Geist, der Jakob überfällt, der Zug begegnet häufig in Märchen. Vgl. Claus Westermann, Genesis, 2. Teilband, Genesis 12-36, BK I/2, Neukirchen 1989, 629.

sehr unterschiedliche Antworten.[60] In symbol-psychologischer Deutung hingegen wird davon ausgegangen, dass Jakob mit seinem archetypischen Schatten-Bruder rang. Nach Carl Gustav Jung ist der Schatten der inferiore Teil der Persönlichkeit und der kollektiven psychischen Dispositionen, die infolge ihrer Unvereinbarkeit mit der bewusst gewählten Lebensform nicht gelebt werden und sich zu einer relativ autonomen Teilpersönlichkeit mit konkreten Tendenzen im Unbewussten zusammenschließen.[61] Deshalb sind die wichtigsten Aufgaben des Menschen überhaupt das Akzeptieren des Schattens und die Integration des Animus oder der Anima.[62] Die Lebensmitte wird dabei als Zeitraum erfahren, der dies geradezu erzwingt, weil die Mechanismen der Unterdrückung nicht mehr grundsätzlich funktionieren bzw. an Gewicht verlieren. [63]

Esau kann also als Jakobs Schattenseite betrachtet werden, und der nächtliche Kampf am Jabbok ist dann nichts anderes als ein Versuch, diese Schattenseite zu integrieren. Jakobs Kampf ist ein Kampf, den er gegen sich selbst führt. Als Jakob seine dunkle Seite akzeptieren kann, gibt das Gegenüber sich als Gott zu erkennen. Das Kämpfen um die eigene Ganzheit und das Annehmen des Schattens führt in die Gotteserfahrung, in die tiefste, nämlich religiöse Dimension menschheitlicher Erfahrung.[64] Jakob erfährt, dass er nicht nur in die Tiefen seines individuellen Lebens hinabgestiegen ist, sondern in die Tiefe, in der Gott erreichbar ist.

Seinen Namen nennt der Unbekannte nicht[65], aber er fragt nach Jakobs Namen. Der Segnende muss den Namen des Segensempfängers kennen, denn der Segen wird einer bestimmten Person zugesprochen. Wie der blinde Isaak in Gen 27,18 nach dem Namen dessen fragt, den er vorhat zu segnen, so fragt hier der Unbekannte nach dem Namen

60 Nach Westermann »ist es nicht JHWH gewesen oder der Gott seines Vaters, der Jakob an der Furt überfallen hat, sondern der Flussdämon, der ihn am Übergang hindern wollte« (Claus Westermann, Genesis, 2. Teilband, Genesis 12-36, BK I/2, 635.). Josef Scharbert, Genesis 12-50, NEB, Würzburg 1986, 222; Terence E. Fretheim, The Book of Genesis, The New Interpreter's Bible, I., Nashville 1994, 567 und Jochen Boecker, 1 Mose 25,12–37,1, Isaak und Jakob, ZBK 1,3, 103, meinen in dem »Mann« Gott selbst zu erkennen.

61 Vgl. Helmut Hark, Der Traum als Gottes vergessene Sprache, 45.

62 Vgl. Carl Gustav Jung, Az élet delén. In: M. Bodrog (szerk.) Mélységeink ösvényein. Gondolat 1930, Budapest 1993.

63 Aufbau der Existenz, Familiengründung etc.

64 Vgl. Renate Klein, Jakob, Wie Gott auf krummen Linien gerade schreibt, 209.

65 Vgl. Ri 13,18.

dessen, der den Segen begehrt.[66] Jakob selber wird gezwungen, seinen Namen zu nennen, sich als den zu erkennen, der er tatsächlich ist. Indem er seinen Namen nennt, sucht er nicht mehr das Gelingen seines Lebens durch die Unterdrückung seiner negativen Anteile zu sichern, sondern setzt sich seinem Schatten aus, den dunklen Seiten seines Wesens, die so aus der Verdrängung zurückgeholt werden. Das Fluchtsymbol verwandelt sich in das der Heimkehr zu sich selbst, mit der Rückkehr aus der Fremde ist die Selbstentfremdung aufgehoben.[67]

Der Angreifer berührt Jakob an der Hüfte, so dass dieser fortan hinkt. Diese Berührung von Gott hat eine große Bedeutung, denn er wird immer mit den Spuren des Kampfes behaftet bleiben.[68] Jakob kann nicht mehr zu schrankenloser Machterweiterung des Ich ausschreiten. Die Berührung Gottes hat bleibende Folgen, mit der Wandlung Jakobs werden die reiferen Dimensionen erkennbar, die Stationen der Menschenwerdung.

In Gen 32 ist Jakob im Kampf der Nacht ein anderer geworden, ein wahrhaft Gesegneter, dem Gott das eigenmächtige Verfügen-Wollen über Segen und Leben abgerungen hat. Die Wandlung Jakobs ist zwar ein innerer Prozeß, nach Gen 32 aber nicht denkbar ohne göttliches Eingreifen bzw. sein souveränes Handeln.[69]

6 Konklusionen

Die Auseinandersetzung in Gen 32 findet nicht nur durch einen Kampf mit dem Bruder Esau statt, sondern mit Gott, denn dieser Konflikt berührt den Punkt, an dem die menschliche Unzulänglichkeit Jakobs an das Unendliche, die unverfügbare Ganzheit stößt.[70]

Im Kampf am Jabbok gelingt Jakob die Identifikation mit seinem Schatten-Bruder. Er konnte sein Ich-Bewusstsein in der Auseinandersetzung bewahren, erlangte den Segen und erhielt einen neuen Namen. Wenn Jakob zu seinem Gegner sagt: »Ich lasse dich nicht, es sei denn, du segnest mich«, erkämpft er sich dessen Segen. Die

[66] Vgl. Hans Jochen Boecker, 1 Mose 25,12-37,1, Isaak und Jakob, ZBK 1,3, 102.
[67] Vgl. Maria Kassel, Biblische Urbilder, 275.
[68] Vgl. Hermann Spieckermann, Der Gotteskampf: Jakob und der Engel in Bibel und Kunst, Zürich 1997, 20.
[69] Vgl. Hermann Spieckermann, Der Gotteskampf, 91-92.
[70] Vgl. Maria Kassel, Biblische Urbilder, 272.

Ganzheitserfahrung des Segens kommt in der Namensänderung zum Ausdruck. Jakob wird Israel, »Gottesstreiter«, genannt.[71]

Jetzt erhält er einen neuen Namen: »Israel«. Der Name wird so erklärt: »Du hast mit Gott und mit Menschen gekämpft und hast gewonnen«. »Mit Menschen« kann sich hier nur darauf beziehen, dass Jakob mit seinem Schatten gekämpft hat. Dieser Satz besagt, dass Gott da zu erfahren ist, wo der Mensch in hartem Ringen, durch Annahme der abgewehrten dunklen Seite, die dissoziierten Lebenskräfte in Ausgleich zu bringen vermag. Einswerden mit sich selbst, Selbstannahme, damit auch die Annahme der abgelehnten Seiten der eigenen Person, schafft die Möglichkeit der Gotterfahrung.[72] In der Versöhnung mit Esau beginnt der Individuationsprozess durch die Konfrontation mit sich selbst im Lichte der Gottesbegegnung.

In der Geschichte Jakobs haben die Träume eine wichtige Rolle, der Traum gehört zur Ganzheit des Lebens und der Gottesbeziehung. Die Quelle der Ganzheitserfahrung ist der Traum. Im Traum von der Himmelsleiter erfährt Jakob bei Bethel, dass der Verkehr zwischen Erde und göttlicher Welt möglich ist; so wird das Symbol der Leiter zur Brücke und zum Mittler zwischen dem Ich-Bewusstsein und dem umfassenden großen Du.[73]

Der Segen steht ganz am Ende des nächtlichen Ringens, jetzt ist es kein Ergebnis der Forderung Jakobs mehr, jetzt ist er reine Gabe, nicht durch ihn selbst herausgefordert. Jakob ist durch den Kampf zu einem Menschen geworden, der weiß, dass er sich nicht sich selbst verdankt.

Der eigenartige und ohne den in Gen 32 vorausgehenden Konflikt unverständliche Satz »ich sah dein Angesicht, als sähe ich Gottes Angesicht« (Gen 33,10) belegt, dass der Kampf mit dem unbekannten göttlichen Wesen und die Auseinandersetzung mit Esau archetypisch in gleicher Weise die Schattenproblematik Jakobs beschreibt und dass die in der Begegnung mit Esau abgebildete Versöhnung mit der eigenen dunklen Tiefe als Erfahrung Gottes verstanden wird.[74]

Jakob ist schmerzhaft an seine Grenze gestoßen, die er aber als das Tor zu der ihn umgreifenden Dimension des Unbedingten, hinein in die Dimension Gottes erfahren hat.

71 Vgl. Helmut Hark, Der Traum als Gottes vergessene Sprache, 47.
72 Vgl. Maria Kassel, Biblische Urbilder, 275.
73 Vgl. Helmut Hark, Der Traum als Gottes vergessene Sprache, 62.
74 Vgl. Kassel, Biblische Urbilder, 279.

Was sich zunächst tiefenpsychologisch als eine innerfamiliär bestimmte Entwicklung und Erfahrung darstellt, wird schließlich transzendiert und zu einem wesentlichen Moment der Gotteserfahrung.

Familie und Verwandtschaft: Wer kümmert sich heute um die Familie?

Übt Gehorsamkeit und Liebe (in der Familie) denn

das ist wohlgefällig dem Herrn. (Kolosser 3,18–4,1)

Zsolt Geréb

1 Aktualität des Themas

Nach biblischer Auffassung gehört die Familie zu den Schöpfungsordnungen (Gen 2,24). Diese Lehre wird sowohl von Jesus, als auch vom Apostel Paulus vertreten (Markus 10,7; 1Kor 11,7). Die Familie bildet den kleinsten Kern sowohl des Volkes Gottes im Alten Testament, als auch der christlichen Kirche, aber auch der Gesellschaft. Diese biblische Anschauung hat das Ethos des Familienlebens im Umfeld der christlichen Kirchen in Mittel-und Osteuropa bis in die neueste Zeit bestimmt. Seit der politischen Wende von 1989 ist das herkömmliche Familienbild verändert. Wenn man die diesbezüglichen Untersuchungen von Soziologen, und die jährlichen Synodalberichte der Landeskirchen liest, stellt man erstens fest, dass viele junge Männer und Frauen allein leben, oder erst spät eine Familie gründen. Zweitens sehen wir, dass sich ein Drittel der geschlossenen Ehen nach kurzem Zusammensein auflöst. Drittens: eine nicht geringe Zahl von jungen Eltern verlassen ihre Kinder, oder stellen sie unter die Obhut der Großeltern, um dann jahrelang im Ausland Gastarbeit zu verrichten. Diese Beobachtungen zeigen uns zuerst, dass die Familie nicht mehr die ideale Lebensform für die junge Generation ist, zweitens dass Treue und gegenseitiges Engagement zwischen den Ehepartnern nicht mehr so dauerhaft ist, wie vor einigen Jahrzehnten.

Angesichts dieser negativen Erscheinungen müssen wir Theologen uns fragen, welche Faktoren diese Veränderungen ausgelöst haben? Meiner Meinung nach sind diese Gründe in dem Prozess der Säkularisation zu suchen. Die früher als göttlich anerkannten Werte und Strukturen haben ihre Autorität und Anziehungskraft verloren, die Interessen der Individuen sind wichtiger geworden als die einer Gemeinschaft. Das Nachlassen des ehelichen Verantwortungsgefühls und der Schwund des gegenseitigen Respekts in der Familie sind als eine Folge des Glaubensverlustes anzusehen. Der säkularisierte Mensch ist entfremdet vom biblischen Familienethos, weil sein Verhältnis zu Gott und zu seinen Mitmenschen wegen seiner autonomen und egozentrischen Lebensziele gefährdet ist.

Was können wir in einer Zeit der Transformation der moralischen Werte tun? Es ist nötig, dass wir der apologetische Methode der nachapostolischen Zeit folgen in der Weise, dass wir auf bleibende Werte der biblischen Botschaft hinweisen. Was haben die urchristlichen Lehrer in dem sich wandelnden Kontext der heidnischen Kultur getan? Sie haben die christlichen Strukturen an die antiken hellenistischen Strukturen adaptiert. Sie haben die sozialen Strukturen der Antike angenommen in der Weise, dass sie ihnen einen christlichen Charakter verliehen haben. Für diese Anpassung liefern die neutestamentlichen Haustafeln ein gutes Beispiel. Die Apostelschüler haben die Gattung Haustafel aus der Ökonomie-Literatur übernommen, aber zugleich dieser ethischen Form einen genuin christlichen Inhalt gegeben.

In diesem Beitrag möchte ich die christlichen Charakterzüge der kolossischen Haustafeln untersuchen in ihrem Verhältnis zur antiken Ökonomie-Literatur.

2 Analyse

Im Kolosserbrief haben wir die erste christliche Haustafel vor uns.[1] Diese paränetische Gattung ist im Neuen Testament im Epheserbrief (5,21–6,9), im ersten Petrusbrief (1Pt 2,13–3,2), sowie später in der Didache (4,9–11) weiterentwickelt worden. »Der Terminus Haustafel ist eine Liste der verschiedenen Pflichten und Verantwortlichkeiten, die für die Mitglieder einer Hausgemeinschaft gelten. Solche Listen erscheinen

[1] P. Pokorny / U. Heckel, Einleitung in das Neue Testament, Tübingen 2007, Exkurs 11, Haustafeln, 635-37.

in ethischen Schriften der Antike und beinhalten das angemessene Verhalten gegenüber den Göttern, dem Staat, den Freunden, anderen Mitgliedern der Hausgemeinschaft und Außenstehenden. Inhalt, Form und Funktion variieren sehr stark.«[2] Nach allgemeiner Auffassung muss die Quelle der Haustafeln in den ethischen Schriften der stoischen Philosophie gesucht werden.[3] Die Forscher berufen sich besonders auf die Schriften von Epiktetos (Diss. II. 17,31). Einst wandte sich ein edler Jüngling an den Philosophen mir der Frage: »Ich möchte wissen, mit was für Pflichten ich als frommer Mensch und Philosoph den Göttern, Eltern, Brüdern, Freunden, Fremden und der Heimat gegenüber schuldig bin?« Der Meister führt in seiner Antwort aus, was Göttern, Eltern, Brüdern, Freunden, Fremden und der Heimat nach der Lehre von der stoischen Selbstbeherrschung gebührt. Die Lehre bezieht sich auf die Männer: »Ich darf nicht so unempfindlich sein wie eine Statue, sondern muss diejenigen natürlichen Beziehungen pflegen, in denen ich als frommer Mensch, Sohn, Bruder, Bürger lebe« (Diss. III. 2.4). Die Haustafeln hatten ein gewisses Schema, das in konkreten Fällen in Bezug auf verschieden Situationen und Zwecke geändert werden konnte.[4] Dieses Verhaltensprinzip wurde von den popularphilosophischen Lehrern des ersten Jahrhunderts übernommen, und spiegelt sich hauptsächlich in den Schriften von Polybios, Stobaios (Hierokles) wider. Die Lehre der hellenistischen Popularphilosophie zur Zeit Jesu wirkte stark auf das Diasporajudentum. Der Autor des Kolosserbriefes (Timotheus) hatte die literarische Gattung der Haustafeln durch die Vermittlung des hellenistischen Judentums kennengelernt. Die Gattung wurde, vom Wort *oikos* (Haus), Ökonomie genannt, d.h. Lehre von der Verwaltung des Hauses. Es ist charakteristisch für die Ökonomie-Literatur, dass der Adressat immer der Hausherr ist, der als Haupt der Familie den übrigen Familienmitgliedern gegenübersteht. Die angeführten Weisungen dienen dem pragmatischen Zweck, die Verwaltung des Hauses reibungslos und mit großer wirtschaftlicher Wirksamkeit zu betreuen.[5]

In meinen Beitrag möchte ich auf die christlichen Charakterzüge der kolossischen Haustafeln hinweisen in ihrer Beziehung zur antiken Ökonomie-Literatur.

2 J.T. Fitzgerald, Artikel Haustafel, in: RGG[4], Bd. 3, 1485.f.

3 D. Lürmann, Neutestamentliche Haustafeln und antike Ökonomie, NTS 27 (1981) 83-97; W. Schrage, Zur Ethik der ntl. Haustafeln, NTS 21 (1975) 1-22.

4 J. Gnilka, Der Kolosserbrief, Exkurs 3, Freiburg 1980, 211.

5 U. Luz, Der Brief an die Kolosser. NTD Bd. 8/1, Göttingen 1998, 235

Die urchristlichen Haustafeln unterscheiden sich von der hellenistischen Ökonomie-Literatur in erster Linie dadurch, dass nicht nur der Hausherr, sondern alle Mitglieder der Familie, bzw. des Haushaltes Adressaten der Paränese sind. Das ist in der Tatsache begründet, dass die Mitglieder der urchristlichen Hausgemeinden gemeinsam und alle an den Gottesdiensten teilgenommen haben oder: teilnahmen hatten.[6] Ihre geistliche Eigenart besteht darin, dass alle Adressaten der Haustafeln *in Christus* sind und ihm verantwortlich sind, ohne Rücksicht darauf, ob sie von ihrem gesellschaftlichen Rang her dem Hausherrn unter- oder übergeordnet sind. Die Adressaten sind vorwiegend im städtischen in städtischem Raum lebende Hausgemeinden, die Lebens- und Konsumgemeinschaften bilden. Die literarische Form der Ermahnungen an die Hausgemeinschaften hatte sich in der urchristlichen Kirche eingebürgert, weil die Gemeinden größtenteils aus Mitgliedern derselben Familie gebildet waren. Die Apostelgeschichte und der erste Korintherbrief berichten davon, dass nach der Bekehrung des Familienoberhauptes das ganze Haus getauft wurde (Apg 16,15.31–34; 18,8; 1Kor 1,16; 16,15). Ähnlich steht es im Brief an Philemon, in dem der *pater familias* ermahnt wird, mit dem Sklaven wie mit einem Bruder umzugehen (Philem. 16). Der besondere Zug der christlichen Haustafeln besteht darin, dass die Mitglieder der Familien bzw. der Hausgemeinschaften nicht bloß durch natürlich menschliche Empfindungen, sondern durch *Liebe* miteinander verbunden waren.[7]

In der folgenden Auslegung möchte ich meine Aufmerksamkeit auf die oben genannten Charakterzüge richten, um das Bild der christlichen Familie zu zeichnen.

3 Auslegung

Das Verhältnis der Ehegatten (3,18–19)

Der Apostel redet zuerst die Frauen an. Sie werden ermahnt, ihrem Mann gegenüber gehorsam zu sein. Dem heutigen Leser wird darin vor allem die untergeordnete Stellung auffallen. In der Bibel ist die

[6] U. Wilckens, Theologie des Neuen Testaments. Bd. I. Teilband 3. Neukirchener 2005, 263.

[7] J. Bolyki, Újszövetségi etika (Ethik des Neuen Testaments), Budapest 1998, 143.

Gleichberechtigung im heutigen Sinne nicht zu finden. Bei Paulus wird der Vorrang der Männer mit der Schöpfungsordnung begründet (1Kor 11,7; 1Mose 2,18). Interessanterweise spricht der Verfasser des Kolosserbriefes in Vers 3,11 nicht über die Aufhebung der Unterscheidung zwischen Mann und Frau innerhalb der christlichen Gemeinde wie das Paulus in seinem Brief an die Galater tut (Gal. 3,28). In dieser Hinsicht teilt der Verfasser des Kolosserbriefes nicht die Anschauung des Apostels. Von den antiken Autoren sprechen unter anderen Aristoteles (Pol. I. 5, 1) und Plutarch (Praec Coniug 11, 19) über diese Frage. Laut Aristoteles stammt das ungleiche Verhältnis zwischen den zwei Geschlechtern aus der naturgegebenen Schwäche der Frauen. Der griechische Philosoph gibt aber zu, dass der Vergleich oft zugunsten der Frauen ausfällt (Pol. I. 5,1). Über diesen Wechsel der Rollen können wir auch im Alten Testament lesen, wenn wir z. B. an Deborah denken, die im Buch der Richter »Mutter Israels« genannt wird (5,7). Der Verfasser verwendet zum Ausdruck des Gehorsams das Verb *hypotassō* (hier Passivum), was nicht Unterworfenheit, sondern Unterordnung bezeichnet.[8] Nach Delling entspricht diese Unterordnung dem Willen Gottes, der die Frau nach dem Manne geschaffen hat, damit sie ihm eine Hilfe sei (1Mos. 3,16; 1Petr 3,5–6). Dieser Gehorsam hat freiwilligen Charakter, man denke auch an die Unterordnung Jesu unter Gott (1Kor 15,28) und genauso Sara ihrem Manne, Abram (1Kor 11,3.7; 14,34). Der Verfasser motiviert die Ermahnung mit den Worten: *wie es sich gehört in dem Herrn.* »In dieser Begründung stehen die hellenistische gesellschaftliche Konvention und die christliche Anschauung nebeneinander. Der Ausdruck: »wie es sich gehört« entspricht dem stoischen *kathēkon*-Begriff, der ebenfalls zur Bezeichnung »der jeweiligen Pflicht« diente.[9] Der christlichen Frau ist diese Pflicht als Folge ihres Gottesverhältnisses (Verbundenheit) auferlegt worden«.[10] Diese Gehorsamkeit ist etwas ganz Anderes als die Unterordnung der Kinder und Sklaven (1Petr 2,18 und 3,1). Das Leben *in dem Herrn* bestimmt sowohl das gottesdienstliche als auch das gesellschaftliche Verhalten und das Familienleben eines Christen. Man akzeptiert Gottes

8 Delling Art. *Hypotassō* TWNT IX. 40-47.; J.G. Dunn, The Epistles to Colossians and Philemon, NIGTC, Eerdmans 1996, 247.

9 H. Hübner, An Philemon, an die Kolosser, an die Epheser. HNT 12. Mohr Siebeck. 1997. Exkurs: Zum Problem der Haustafeln, 110. Ed. Schweizer, Der Brief an die Kolosser, EKK, Berlin 1979, 164.

10 Sándor Cserháti, Erklärung des Kolosserbriefes und des Philemonbriefes. Budapest 1978, 152.

Willen nicht nur im kultischen Bereich, sondern in verschiedenen Situationen des alltäglichen Lebens. Das Prinzip einer solchen Lebensführung bezieht sich gleichmäßig auf alle Mitglieder einer Familiengemeinschaft. Der Apostel ermahnt die Männer, ihre Frauen zu lieben und gegen sie nicht bitter zu sein. Nach Kol 3,14 ist *die Liebe* das Band, das Mitglieder der Gemeinde miteinander verbindet. Das gilt auch in einer Familiengemeinschaft. Die Väter dürfen ihre Vorrangstellung in der Familie nicht missbrauchen, denn sie leben im Herrn, dessen Gebot gegenüber allen natürlichen, bzw. soziologischen, gesellschaftlichen Konventionen Vorrang hat. Als *patres familias* müssen sie ihre Pflichten mit Mäßigkeit erfüllen, ohne mürrisch und bitter gegen ihre Frauen zu sein.[11] Heute würden wir sagen, dass zwischen den Ehegatten ein humanes, gütiges Verhältnis herrschen muss. Interessanterweise benutzt die hellenistische Literatur den Ausdruck *agapē* nicht in Bezug auf das Verhältnis der Ehegatten. Die stoischen Autoren verwenden in diesen Zusammenhang des Verb *phileĩ*.[12] Zu Jesu Zeiten hielt nicht einmal das Judentum die Liebe für eine erste Bedingung der Ehe.[13] Dennoch treffen wir im Alten Testament an vielen Stellen eine fast literarisch schöne Äußerung der Liebe im Rahmen des Familienlebens (z.B. in der Geschichte von Isaak und Jakob: 1Mose 24,67; 29,18). Diese gefühlsmäßige Einstellung wird zuerst vom Verfasser des Epheserbriefes christologisch begründet (Eph. 5,25).

Das Gegenteil der Liebe ist das mürrische, bittere, rücksichtslose Verhalten. Das wird mit dem Verb *pikrainō* ausgedrückt, das sich von *stichig* herleitet. Das in übertragenem Sinne benutzte Verb weist auf eine abweisende Haltung des Mannes gegenüber seiner Frau hin, und dass er mit ihr das Zwiegespräch unterbricht.[14] Dessen Gegenteil ist die Eintracht (concordia) d. h. das liebevolle Verhalten. Der Verfasser des Briefes betonte damit die Verantwortung des Mannes in der Gestaltung des Ehelebens der Christen.[15] Die Liebe ist ein Mittel, wodurch die in der Welt herrschende Ordnung, die weltlichen Sitten und Bräuche in

[11] A. Lindemann, Der Kolosserbrief, Zürcher Bibelkommentare NT 10. Zürich 1983, 65.

[12] E. Stauffer, Art. Agapēin: TWNT I, 651.

[13] W. Grundmann, Das palästinische Judentum in Zeitraum zwischen der Erhebung der Makkabäer und dem Ende des Jüdischen Krieges. In: J. Leipold und W. Grundmann, Umwelt des Urchristentums, Berlin 1965, 143-291.

[14] Michaelis, Art. Pikrainōin: TWNT VI. 124-125; P. Pokorny, Der Brief des Paulus an die Kolosser ThHK 10/1, Berlin 1987, 153.

[15] P. Pokorny, Kolosserbrief, 153.

den Dienst des neuen Lebens gestellt werden können.[16] Es ist zu bemerken, dass die gegenseitig erwiesene Liebe am rechtlichen Status der Frau nichts ändert, denn sie bleibt im Verhältnis zu ihrem Mann, diesem weithin untergeordnet. Für den Verfasser war die reelle Lage der Familienmitglieder vor Gott wichtiger als ihre soziologisch-gesellschaftliche Konstellation. Vor Gott zählt allein die Liebe.[17]

Die Beziehung zwischen Kindern und Eltern (3,20–21)

Die Beziehung zwischen Kindern und Eltern beruht auf Gegenseitigkeit. Die Tatsache, dass der Apostel die Kinder als besondere Entität anredet zeigt, dass er ihr individuelles Sein anerkennt, was in der antiken Gesellschaft nicht eindeutig war. Nach hellenistischer Auffassung war das Kind noch unreif und konnte nicht zur Rechenschaft gezogen werden. Es muss unter allen Umständen seinen Eltern gehorsam sein. Genauso bedingungslos muss auch der Sklave seinem Herrn gehorchen (v. 22). Das bedeutet nicht nur Unterordnung, sondern völlige Verneinung des selbständigen Handelns und Entscheidens. Das Kind ist auf Bevormundung, auf die Führung von seiner Eltern angewiesen. Mit dieser streng pädagogischen Einstellung war ein gewisser rationaler Optimismus verbunden.[18] Die Eltern betrachteten das Kind als »Rohmaterial«, das durch strenge Erziehung geformt werden kann, das heißt, es kann daraus ein erwachsener Mensch gemeißelt werden. Die Forderung des Gehorsams entsprach dem Willen Gottes (Ex 20,12). Darauf bezieht sich die Begründung dieser Mahnung: *denn das ist dem Herrn gefällig*. Das Gesetz Mose sieht im Ungehorsam den Eltern gegenüber eine Todsünde. Jünglinge, die sich dem Willen ihrer Väter widersetzt haben, konnten von den Ältesten zur Steinigung verurteilt werden (Deut 21,18–21). In Vergleich dazu war die Lehre Jesu bzw. des Kolosserbriefes über das Verhältnis zwischen Kindern und Erwachsenen ein Fortschritt (Mk 10,14–16).[19] Der Begriff *euareston* bedeutet: angenehm, wohlgefällig.[20] Diese Tugend entspricht vor allem der bürgerlichen Ethik, die von Epiktetos vertreten wurde.[21] Dieser

[16] W. Schrage, Ethik des Neuen Testaments. NTD Ergänzungsreihe 4, Göttingen 1989, 258.
[17] H. Hübner, An die Kolosser, 111.
[18] J. Gnilka, Der Kolosserbrief, 219.
[19] A. Lindemann, Der Kolosserbrief, 65.
[20] W. Bauer, Wörterbuch zum NT. 5. Aufl. Berlin. 1963. 630.
[21] Epiktet, Diss. 1, 13, 2; 2, 10. 7

Ausdruck ist auch in den Paulusbriefen zu finden (Röm 12,1; 14,18; Phil 4,18). Das ist ein Hinweis darauf, dass das Neue Testament gesellschaftliche Ordnungsprinzipien des ersten Jahrhunderts angenommen hat. Die christliche Kirche hat aber diese Konvention uminterpretiert, in unserem Fall auf die Weise, dass sie die Persönlichkeit der Kinder anerkennt. Darauf weist der Ausdruck *im Herrn* hin. Durch diese Formel möchte der Verfasser klar machen, dass die Kinder zur Kirche Christi gehören, indem sie die Worte der Eltern befolgen, ihnen gehorchen. In den Zehn Geboten bezieht sich das fünfte auf die Ehrung der Eltern (Ex 20,12; Deut 5,16; Sir 3,1f). Nach der Auffassung des Alten Testaments vertreten die Eltern vor ihren Kindern den Herrn selbst. Auf Ihn, auf die Ihm gebührende Ehre bezieht sich aber das erste Gebot als Zeugnis von Gott, dem befreienden Herrn, der sein Volk aus der ägyptischen Gefangenschaft herausgeführt hat. Die Ehrfurcht der Kinder den Eltern gegenüber ist zugleich ein Ausdruck ihrer Gottesfurcht (*pietas*).

Der zweite Teil der Doppelmahnung wendet sich an die Väter. Von den beiden Eltern waren die Väter verantwortlich für die Erziehung der Kinder. Sie gehörten zum Rechtsbereich der *patria potestas.*[22] Dieses Recht gab dem Familienoberhaupt die Macht, als Rechtsperson zu handeln, seinen Willen in der Hausgemeinde mit Gewalt durchzusetzen. Zugleich war er verpflichtet, seine Familie gegen die Gewalt der Außenwelt zu verteidigen. Hinsichtlich der Kindererziehung ermahnt aber der Apostel die Väter zur Selbstbeherrschung und bittet sie darum, ihre Kinder nicht zu verbittern, auf dass sie nicht mutlos werden. Missbraucht der Vater seine Macht und geht mit seinem Elternrecht taktlos um, so macht er sein in der Entwicklung befindliches Kind schüchtern und lähmt die Entfaltung seiner Persönlichkeit. Weil das Kind vor Gott eine persönliche Identität hat, gebührt ihm eine würdige Behandlungsweise und Elternliebe (*caritas*). Die Härte der Eltern darf das Erwachen des Gottvertrauens im Herzen des Kindes nicht verhindern. Die freundliche Haltung Jesu den Kindern gegenüber hat wahrscheinlich zur Entwicklung dieser Anschauung beigetragen (Mk 10,13–16). In der hellenistischen Literatur finden wir ähnliche Mahnungen, wo die Eltern zur Schonung ihrer Kinder ermahnt werden

[22] Péter Balla, The Child-Parents Relationship in the New Testament and its Environment. WUNT 155. Mohr Siebeck. 2003. 41-58; Christina Urban, Die Rollen der Familienmitgliedern, in: Klaus Scherberich (Hrsg.), Neues Testament und Antike Kultur. Bd. 2. Familie, Gesellschaft, Wirtschaft. Neukirchener 2005, 17-20.

(z.B. Plutarch, Lib. Educ. 12 (II./8F); Menander (Stob Ecl IV. 26. 3–5).[23] Diese pädagogische Anschauung steht bereits der modernen Kinderpsychologie nahe.

Das Verhältnis von Knecht und Herr (Kol 3,22–4,1)

Die dritte Doppelermahnung redet die Knechte und die Herren an. Die Bedeutung des Problems wird dadurch betont, dass die Mahnung an die Knechte am längsten ist.[24] Wie ist das zu erklären? Für den antiken Menschen war das Recht und die menschliche Würde der Sklaven ein anthropologisches und soziologisches Problem von grundlegender Bedeutung.[25] Viele Philosophen beschäftigten sich mit der Frage, warum manche Menschen ohne irgendeine Schuld zu haben, ihre Freiheit, Bewegungs- und Persönlichkeitsrechte verlieren und aus dieser Situation nur selten heraustreten können. Sowohl hellenistische als auch jüdische Denker und Führer haben die Unrechtmäßigkeit der Situation eingesehen, doch machten sie keine konkreten Vorschläge für die Änderung des gesellschaftlichen Status der Sklaven. Auch Jesus und Paulus haben die Situation nicht ändern wollen. Man erklärt den Standpunkt des Apostels mit seiner eschatologischen Anschauung. Nach dem ersten Korintherbrief empfiehlt er den Sklaven deshalb nicht ihre soziale Lage zu ändern, weil in der Hoffnung auf die bevorstehende Wiederkunft die Frage, ob jemand zum Stand der Sklaven oder der Freien gehörte, ihre entscheidende Bedeutung verlor (1Kor 7,20–24).

Der Kolosserbrief widmet mehr Aufmerksamkeit der sozialen Lage der Christen. Wahrscheinlich hatte der Briefschreiber mit einer längeren Wartezeit gerechnet. Für die christliche Gemeinde war es deshalb notwendig geworden, ihr Verhältnis zur Außenwelt theologisch, aber auch unter ethischem Gesichtspunkt zu klären. Während sie die politische Realität der antiken Gesellschaft akzeptierte, wollte sie den sozialen Rahmen, in dem man lebte, menschlicher, humaner gestalten. Hier sehen wir, wie die Kirche des ersten Jahrhunderts ihre sozialethischen Reflexion, ihre Lehre gemäß dem Evangelium entfaltete (Siehe: Eph 6,5–6; 1Pt 2,18–25).

[23] Hinweis nach Ed. Schweizer, Kolosserbrief, 166/ Anm 612, 615

[24] Rengstorf, Art. *doulos oftalmodoulia* in: TWNT I, 275-283.

[25] H. Hübner, Kolosserbrief, 113

Diese Ermahnung zeugt von dieser Bestrebung. Es ist bemerkenswert, dass der Apostel auch die Sklaven genauso wie die Kinder, als persönliche Entitäten anredet. Durch diese Anrede wird ihre Identität, ihre menschliche Würde und persönliche Verantwortung hervorgehoben. Der Verfasser wendet sich mit der Aufforderung an sie, ihren leiblichen Herrn gegenüber in allen Dingen gehorsam zu sein. Der Briefschreiber ordnet auch die Sklaven in allen Dingen dem Willen ihrer Herrn unter. Diese völlige Abhängigkeit wird vom Apostel durch die Einfügung von drei Wörtchen – kata sarka kyriois = ihren leiblichen Herrn – relativiert.[26] So bekommt der Sklavenstand bzw. das Abhängigkeitsverhältnis einen bloß zeitlichen Charakter, wie auch die Befehle der leiblichen Herrn in Vergleich mit dem Gebot des himmlischen Vaters nur provisorisch gelten. Auch für die Knechten ist nicht mehr der Wille ihrer Besitzer das höchste Maß (Apg 5,29). Bemerkenswert ist die Mahnung zum bewussten Dienst: »*nicht mit Dienst vor Augen, als den Menschen zu gefallen, sondern mit Einfalt des Herzens und mit Gottesfurcht*«. Diese Aufforderung bezieht sich auf die geistliche Einstellung der Knechte. Menschen zu gefallen wäre nur äußerlicher Schein, dagegen sollte die gewissenhafte Arbeit der Sklaven die Anerkennung des Herrn anstreben (Eph 6,6), nicht das Lob des leiblichen Herrn, sondern das des himmlischen Herrn suchen. Mit der Einfalt des Herzens und mit Gottesfurcht sollten sie ihren leiblichen Herrn dienen. Diese Mahnung kommt auch bei den neutestamentliche Apokryphen vor (Weisheit Salomos 1,1). Der Ausdruck *haplotēs* bezeichnet Einfalt bzw. Aufrichtigkeit, und mit dem Wort *kardia – Herz* verbunden, bedeutet er offene, aufrichtige Bereitschaft zum Dienst. Diese Haltung steht in Gegensatz zum Verhalten heuchlerischer Menschen.[27] In *der Furcht des Herrn* ist eine eigentümliche alttestamentliche Wendung, die sich in den Bibelstellen Lev 19,14; 25,17 nach LXX, auf ein Fürchten Gottes – d. i. Gottesfurcht – bezieht. Im Neuen Testament bezieht sie sich nicht auf Gott sondern auf den verherrlichten Christus (Off 15,4).[28]

[26] H. Hübner, Kolosserbrief, 113.
[27] R. McI. Wilson, Colossians and Philemon, 283.
[28] Ed Lohse, An die Kolosser, 228.

Kolosser 3,23–24

In den folgenden zwei Versen kommt der Apostel im Allgemeinen auf den Inhalt der vorherigen Ermahnung zurück. Das ist eine Aufforderung alles willig und aus ganzem Herzen zu tun, nicht aus Zwang. Wie kann man einer solchen Aufforderung Folge leisten? So, dass man während des Dienstes auf den himmlischen Herrn und nicht auf den irdischen Herrn schaut.[29] Auf diese Weise werden die Sklaven im Sinne jenes Grundprinzips der christlichen Ethik handeln, das vom Verfasser in Kapitel 3, Vers 17 zusammengefasst wurde: »Alles, was ihr tut mit Worten oder mit Werken, das tut alles in dem Namen des Herrn Jesu und danket Gott und dem Vater durch ihn«. Die Knechte hatten vielerlei niedrige Arbeiten zu leisten. Aber wenn sie während dieser Arbeit »höher« blicken, wird ihre alltägliche Tätigkeit zum Gottesdienst.[30] Dem Ausdruck *ek psychēs – von Herzen* begegnen wir auch im ersten Gebot, das uns auffordert, Gott zu lieben (LXX Deut 6,5; Sirach 6,23; 7, 29). Auch die Weisheitsliteratur kennt die Gegenüberstellung der Gottesfurcht und der Furcht vor Menschen (Sirach 2, 22; 2Sam 24, 14; 1Chr 21, 13: »Wir wollen lieber in die Hände des Herrn fallen als in die Hände der Menschen«). Bei der Begründung des gehorsamen Verhaltens des Knechtes haben wir nicht zu fragen, ob diese Forderung gerecht ist oder nicht, sondern ob er sich zum Dienst des himmlischen Herrn verpflichtet hat.[31] Nach der Aufforderung kommt die Begründung: Ihr werdet die Vergeltung des Erbes von dem Herrn empfangen (V. 24a). Den Sklaven wird empfohlen, ihre Belohnung nicht von ihren leiblichen Herren, sondern von Christus zu erwarten. Zum »Dienst von ganzem Herzen« werden die christlichen Knechte nicht durch die Hoffnung auf Belohnung angespornt, sondern durch den Glauben, Gottes Erben zu werden (Röm 8,17; Gal 5,21; 1Kor 15,20). Aus dieser Motivierung geht in versteckter Weise hervor, dass die Knechte keinen Lohn bekommen hatten. Aber der Hausherr sorgte für die Versorgung der Sklaven. In vielen Fällen hatten sie bessere Lebensbedingungen, als die frei lebenden Armen.[32] Im Alten Testament finden wir Vorschriften, die zur humanen Behandlung der Sklaven ermahnen (Ex 21, 2–6). Aber in der antiken Literatur liest man auch Aufzeichnungen, die das Gegenteil

[29] H. Ridderbos, Aan de Kolossenzen, Kampen 1960, 230.
[30] J. Gnilka, Kolosserbrief, 222.
[31] H. Ridderbos, Kolossenzen, 230.
[32] A. Lindemann, Kolosserbrief, 66; R.Mcl. Wilson, Colossian, 282.

bezeugen.[33] Das Leben der in Bergwerken und auf Plantagen arbeitenden Sklaven war besonders unerträglich.[34] Der Ausdruck *antapodosis – Gegenleistung* kommt im Neuen Testament nur an dieser Stelle vor.[35] In der hellenistischen Literatur bezeichnet dieser Ausdruck in erster Linie die göttliche Strafe (Thucydides), aber in unserem Brief bezieht er sich auf die göttliche Wiedergutmachung, auf den himmlischen Erbschatz, der schon im Himmel vorbereitet ist (siehe Kol 1,5.27; 3,1–4). Niemand soll dieses himmlischen Geschenk verspielen. Die Nachfolger Christi haben danach zu trachten, mit ihrem Dienst dieses Geschenk zu erlangen. Das Wort *Erbe klēronomia* bezog sich in den früheren Büchern des Alten Testaments auf das Land Kanaan, das von Gott dem Volk Israel versprochen war. Für das spätere Judentum bedeutete die Verheißung des Erbes den Empfang des ewigen Lebens.[36]

Kolosser 3,24b enthält eine Aufforderung: *dient dem Herrn Christus!* Wegen des allgemeinen Charakters dieser Ermahnung gilt sie nicht nur für die Knechte, sondern für alle Mitglieder der Familie. Eine ähnliche Ermahnung ist auch im paränetischen Teil des Römerbriefes zu lesen, die gleichfalls allgemein gültig ist (Röm 12,11). Der verherrlichte Christus wird vom Verfasser *Kyrios* genannt. Er will durch diese Aufforderung den Gemeindemitgliedern zur Kenntnis geben, dass sowohl die Sklaven als auch die Herren der Macht des himmlischen Herrn unterordnet sind. Über ihre Arbeit müssen alle ihm Rechenschaft geben.[37]

Vers 3, 25

Auch diese Ermahnung ist an die Sklaven gerichtet. Sie sollten an ein altes rechtliches Prinzip erinnert werden. Die ungerechte Tat verdient Strafe. Dieses Grundprinzip entspricht dem *ius talionis,* das nicht nur im Alten Testament (Ex 21,23–25), sondern auch für Paulus bekannt war (1Kor 3,17). Sollte dieser Satz dem vorigen Vers widersprechen, wo den Knechten das Erbe versprochen wurde? In beiden Sentenzen ist das jüngste Gericht der Maßstab. Manche Forscher wollen in diesem einen

33 David Hellholm, Die Gattung Haustafel im Kolosser- und Epheserbrief. In: Kolosser-Studien (Hrsg.), Peter Müller, Biblisch-Theologische Studien 103, Neukirchener 2009, 103-128.

34 Géza Alföldi, Römische Sozialgeschichte, Wiesbaden 1985, 65.

35 F. Büchsel, Art. Antapodosis TWNT II, 171.

36 J. Hermann, Art *klēronomia* TWNT III, 768, 775.

37 J. Gnilka, Kolosserbrief, 223.

Satz einen Ausdruck heiligen Rechts sehen.[38] Andere Exegeten meinen, diese Sentenz gehöre in die Gattung der Weisheitssprüche.[39] Wir halten die erste Meinung für richtig, weil die Ermahnung eschatologische Beziehung hat.[40] Es ist aber zu betonen, dass der Apostel den Menschen das Recht auf Rache abspricht, weil er dies Gott überlässt (Röm 12,19): »Rächt euch selber nicht, meine Liebsten, sondern gebt Raum dem Zorn (Gottes), denn es steht geschrieben: Die Rache ist mein, ich will vergelten, spricht der Herr«. Nach J. G. Dunn hatte diese Ermahnung einen doppelten Zweck: Einerseits wollte sie die Knechte ermutigen, damit sie wissen, dass die Herren wegen ihres unmenschlichen Benehmens noch in der Gegenwart, oder am letzten Tage bestraft werden, andererseits machte die Ermahnung die Knechte darauf aufmerksam, mit ihrer Unzufriedenheit die Grenze nicht zu überschreiten.[41] Mit anderen Worten weist der Verfasser darauf hin, dass Christus alle Ungerechtigkeiten bestrafen wird, unabhängig davon ob diese von den Hausherren oder den Knechten begangen wurden. Das wird durch den Satzschluss bestätigt: *es gilt kein Ansehen der Person.* Das Hauptwort *prosϕolϵmpsia* bedeutet *Ansehen der Person.* Im Alten Testament wird dieser Begriff oft benutzt, wo man von Gottes gerechtem Urteil Zeugnis ablegen wollte. Ins Neue Testament gelangte er durch die Vermittlung des hellenistischen Judentums.[42] Das Wort gibt die alttestamentliche Wendung *prosϕon lambanein* wieder (Lev 19,15; Hiob 42,8; Mal 2,9). Die Bedeutung des Begriffes wird klar veranschaulicht in der Ermahnung des Apostels Jakobus (2,1–4). Die Parteilosigkeit des Richters äußert sich so, dass er unter den Menschen keinen Unterschied macht und ohne Voreingenommenheit jeden Menschen nach seinen Taten richtet (Röm 2,11: »es ist kein Ansehen der Person vor Gott«). Die Ermahnungen ermuntern die Christen, die Person jedes Menschen zu respektieren. Der Apostel verurteilt die Menschen die die Sünde der Parteinahme begehen, indem sie aus materiellen oder andere Motiven Einige bevorzugen und Andere nach hinten stellen. Die Christen sollen Gottes Beispiel folgen und über einzelne Menschen und verschiedene Volksgruppen recht urteilen.[43]

38 E. Käsemann, Sätze heiligen Rechtes im Neuen Testaments. In: Exegetische Versuche und Besinnungen II, 1965, 69-82.

39 K. Berger, Zu den sog. Sätzen heiligen Rechtes, NTS 17 (1970), 10-40.

40 P. Pokorny, Kolosserbrief, 155; U. Luz, An die Kolosser, 238.

41 J. G. Dunn, Colossians, 258.

42 Ed. Lohse, Art. *prosōpolēmpsia* in: TWNT VI, 780f.

43 J. G. Dunn, Colossians, 259.

Nach den Familienmitgliedern redet der Apostel den Hausherrn an. Im Gegensatz zu den vorherigen Ermahnungen ist die Kürze dieser Ermahnung auffallend. Dieser Umstand vermindert aber inhaltlich die Bedeutung dieser Mahnung nicht. Die Herren werden ermahnt, mit den Sklaven in ihrem Hause gerecht umzugehen. Es soll ihnen gegeben werden, was ihnen nach dem Recht zusteht: Verpflegung, Kleidung und Unterkunft. Der Hausherr ist der Garant der Gerechtigkeit[44] bzw. der Anwalt des Rechts im Haushalt. Er muss mit seinem Verhalten danach trachten, jede Ungerechtigkeit zu vermeiden.[45] Das Wort *isotēs* bedeutet in diesem Zusammenhang nicht Gleichheit, auch nicht soziale Egalität,[46] sonder *Billigkeit,*[47] das ist gerechte, menschliche Behandlung. Der Verfasser ermahnt durch diese Aufforderung die Herren, vor ihren Entscheidungen die Umstände zu erwägen und den Knechten gegenüber immer wohlwollend zu sein. Er bittet sie, ihre Macht nicht zu missbrauchen und die ausgelieferte Lage der Sklaven nicht auszunutzen. Er macht sie darauf aufmerksam, dass die Normen der Gerechtigkeit und der Billigkeit nicht von ihnen gegeben sind, sondern es gibt einen allgemein anerkannten Maßstab der Korrektheit und Solidarität unter den Menschen.[48]

Dieses entspricht der Goldenen Regel, die nicht nur für das Neue Testament, sondern auch für die stoische Philosophie, bzw. das hellenistische Judentum galt (Mt 7,12: »Was ihr wollt, dass euch die Leute tun sollen, das tut ihr ihnen auch«. – Senecas Brief an Lucilius 47,10–12: »Behandle deine Untergebenen so, wie du es wünschst, dass dein Vorgesetzter dich behandelt. So oft es dir in den Sinn kommt, was alles du deinen Sklaven antun kannst, denke daran, dass dein Herr dir genau so viel antun kann«. – Pseudo-Phokylides 224: »Du sollst dem Sklaven mit einem gehäuften Maß messen«. – Jesus Sirach 7,21: »Du sollst den klugen Knecht so liebhaben, wie deine eigene Seele, verweigere ihm nicht die Freiheit«. In dieser Hinsicht geht der Autor des deuterokanonischen Buches Jesus Sirach, am weitesten, der sogar die Freilassung des Sklaven vorschlägt. Weder der Apostel Paulus noch der Verfasser des Kolosserbriefes empfiehlt den Herren diesen Schritt.

[44] G. Schrenk, Art *dikaios* TWNT II, 189.
[45] J. Gnilka, Kolosserbrief, 224.
[46] G. Stählin, Art *isotēs* TWNT III, 355.
[47] T. Holtz, Art *isos* EWNT II, 495.
[48] J. Gnilka, Kolosserbrief, 225.

Gnilka erklärt dies damit, dass es in der Gemeinde wahrscheinlich nur wenige Sklavenhalter gab.

Auch hier hat die Begründung der Ermahnung eschatologischen bzw. theologischen Charakter. Alles soll im Bewusstsein getan werden, dass der himmlische Herr am letzten Tage alle Menschen zur Verantwortung rufen wird (Vers 25). Die Ermahnung wird durch diese Aussage des Verfassers nicht nur begründet, sondern auch inhaltlich bestimmt. Der Christ, in unserem Fall der christliche Hausherr. hat nicht nur den allgemeinen, menschlichen Gesetzen zu entsprechen, sondern vor allem dem Gesetz Christi, das heißt aber dem Gebot der Liebe, besonders in dem Fall, wo der Knecht zur christlichen Gemeinde gehört (Philem 16).[49] Die Nachfolger Christi tragen größere Verantwortung, weil sie für ihre Taten nicht nur vor dem menschlichen Gericht, sondern auch vor dem Thron des himmlischen Richters antworten werden. Die Perspektive der himmlischen Rechenschaft stellt die Beziehung zwischen Herren und Sklaven in eine neue Beleuchtung. Sie muss Demut erwecken sowohl in den Herren als auch in den Knechten, vor allem durch die gegenseitige Liebe.

Aufs Ganze gesehen ist es unerlässlich zu betonen, dass man die Ermahnungen nicht von ihrem geschichtlichen, sozialen Umfeld, in welchem sie entstanden sind, trennen darf. Diese ethischen Forderungen sind vielleicht fremdartig im Auge des heutigen Menschen, besonders diejenigen Feststellungen, die über das Verhältnis der Sklaven zu ihren Herren handeln. Wenn wir aber diese Mahnungen im Kontext der gegebenen geschichtlichen Zeitperiode betrachten, erscheinen sie uns logisch und natürlich.

Die aktuelle Bedeutung der Haustafeln wird erst dann zum Vorschein kommen, wenn wir diejenigen ethischen Prinzipien erkennen, welche sie bestimmt haben: Respektierung des Nächsten als einer selbständigen Person, Respekt vor anderen Völkern, Übung von Geduld und Verständnis gegenüber kleineren oder größeren gesellschaftlichen Gruppen, Meidung aller Äußerungen, durch welche wir unseren Nächsten Bitternis verursachen. Die Haustafeln ermahnen uns zu einem billigen, gerechten Umgang mit den uns anvertrauten Menschen, zu der Erkenntnis unserer eigenen Rechte und Verantwortungen, und zum Respekt gegenüber Rechten und Interessen von Anderen. Das sind die fundamentalen Prinzipien, auf denen ein

[49] H. Ridderbos, Kolossenzen, 232.

glückliches Familienleben und ein solidarisches Gemeinschaftsleben gebaut werden kann.

Unter den Mahnungen sind einige von allgemeiner Geltung, andere haben einen spezifischen Charakter. Man darf die Situation der einzelnen Gemeinschaften nicht verallgemeinern. Die aktuellen Umständen sind verschieden, je nach geographischem Ort, je nach Zeitperiode und sogar von einem Haushalt zum anderen. Man kann despotischen Hausherren, oder rechthaberischen Vätern begegnen, aber das heißt noch nicht, dass alle Vorgesetzten grausam sind. Oder »man kann rebellische Kinder und Diener antreffen, aber man weiß, dass nicht alle Söhne Revolutionäre sind«[50].

50 Siehe R. Mcl Wilson, Colossian, 287-88; Ed. Schweizer, Kolosserbrief, 169-170; J. Bolyki, Ethik des Neuen Testaments, 124-125.

Families of Strangers

Families in the Dutch Stranger Church

as Examples of Early Modern Families

Henk van den Belt

1 Abstract

According to recent research, the early modern family shows much similarity with the modern family; love and affection determine early modern family relationships. This paper summarizes these newer trends in historical research, especially the contribution of Steven Ozment and tests it against the situation of the families in the Dutch Stranger Church in London. The history of this church is very well documented. From the form of marriage and from the regulation of Christian education it becomes clear that affectionate love was the ideal for the family and that special care was taken for the education of the children. When one compares the liturgical forms with the minutes of the consistory, it is surprising that the forms are silent about the male and female servants that lived with the families. Perhaps their presence was the largest difference between early modern and modern families.

2 New Lines of Research on Early Modern Families

Historians in the 1960s and 1970s argued that medieval and early modern families differed essentially from modern families. The modern family, in the view of the influential authors Philippe Ariès (1914–1984)[1] and Lawrence Stone (1919–1999)[2], was more sentimental. In the patriarchal pre-modern families emotional affection between spouses was still lacking and children were seen as property. According to the often quoted statement of Ariès »in medieval society, the idea of childhood did not exist.«[3] Childhood followed only after the economic and social changes of the seventeenth century. Ariès proved his point by illustrations of children dressed like adults.

Among early modernists these views are no longer authoritative.[4] Criticism of this approach has been expressed since the close of the twentieth century. Ariès, for example, was not aware of the fact that the children on the pictures were put in adult clothes just for the painting of the portraits.[5] On a popular level, however, many people still believe that affection in the family hardly existed before the late eighteenth century.

In his booklet *Ancestors: The Loving Family in Old Europe* (2001), Steven Ozment (1939-) corrects this picture, drawing from twenty years of publications in the field of family history in early modern Germany.[6]

1 His most influential work on the theme is Philippe Ariès, L'enfant et la vie familiale sous l'Ancien Régime. Civilisations d'hier et d'aujourd'hui (Paris: Plon, 1960). English translation Philippe Ariès, Centuries of Childhood; A Social History of Family Life, New York 1962. Ariès is also well known for treatment of the history of attitudes to death and dying, which he also deemed a social construction. Philippe Ariès, L'homme devant la mort: Univers historique, Paris 1977.

2 Stone worked at the University of Oxford (1947-1963) and was professor of history at Princeton University (1963-1990). Using quantitative methods to study family life, Stone concluded that was little love in English marriages before the 18th century. Lawrence Stone, The Family, Sex and Marriage in England, 1500-1800, New York 1977.

3 Ariès, Centuries of Childhood, 125.

4 Diarmaid MacCulloch states that much of the evidence from the French social history school was based on records from elite circles in which inheritance laws often turned marriages into commercial transactions. Diarmaid MacCulloch, Reformation: Europe's House Divided, 1490-1700, London 2003, 597.

5 Richard J. Evans, In Defence of History, London 1997, 63. For a survey of criticisms of Ariès cf. James A. Schultz, ›Medieval Adolescence: The Claims of History and the Silence of German Narrative,‹ in: Speculum 66 (1991), 519-539, 519 n5 and n6.

6 Steven Ozment, Ancestors: The Loving Family in Old Europe, Cambridge 2001. Ozment is one of Heiko A. Oberman's students and has taught in Tübingen and at Yale and Harvard. His previous publications on the family include Steven Ozment, When Fathers Ruled: Family Life in Reformation Europe, Cambridge

He shows that the relationship between spouses was much more loving and cooperative and that affection of parents for children was much deeper than assumed in the critical analyses of the second half of the twentieth century. Over against the view that women were always victims, Ozment cites many cases where women were treated equal to or even had more rights than some men. Whereas children are often portrayed as sufferers of harsh treatment, he shows that many children were not treated badly. Also, practices that may seem cruel and harsh nowadays were simply practical in earlier contexts. Scholars in the second half of the twentieth century often took the modern ethos as a norm to measure history. In short, the picture of the pre-modern family as hierarchical and emotionally crippled is a liberal caricature.

Methodologically, Ozment advocates cooperation between historical and sociological approaches to produce an objective picture. The quantitative evidence from official public records must be balanced by qualitative information from stories, diaries and letters from family archives. Family archives document spousal and parental love and show the same deep bonds of love in marriage and between parents and children which are now associated with the modern ›nuclear family‹. According to Ozment, »such high qualities prove to be specific to family life itself and not to time and place – this notwithstanding the very different public faces that time and place always affix to particular ages and cultures.«[7]

3 *The Liturgy and Church Order of the Dutch Stranger Church*

We will now turn to the documents of the Dutch Stranger Church, to see if we can find love and affection behind that particular face. The Dutch Church in London received a royal charter on July 24, 1550.[8]

1983, and Steven Ozment, Flesh and Spirit: A Study of Private Life in Early Modern Germany, New York 1999.

7 Ozment, Ancestors, 109.

8 On the history of the church cf. J. Lindeboom, Austin Friars: geschiedenis van de Nederlandse Hervormde Gemeente te Londen, 1550-1950, The Hague 1950. English translation J. Lindeboom, Austin Friars: History of the Dutch Reformed Church in London 1550 – 1950, The Hague 1950. Andrew Pettegree, Foreign Protestant Communities in Sixteenth-Century London, Oxford [Oxfordshire] 1986, Peter Grell Ole, Dutch Calvinists in Early Stuart London: The Dutch Church in Austin Friars, 1603-1642, Leiden 1989, O. Boersma, Vluchtig voorbeeld. De nederlandse, franse en italiaanse vluchtelingenkerken in Londen,

Edward VI (1537–1553) donated the church of the Austin Friars to the congregation of Dutch strangers and refugees in the city. The congregation had a superintendent and four pastors, two for the Dutch and two for the Walloon members. The Dutch protestant church had its own organization and liturgy and was independent from the Church of England. The fact that this was allowed was a sign of the Calvinistic character of the Reformation in England at that time. The congregation, that might have had a number of 3.000 to 4.000, consisted of protestant refugees and people from the community of Dutch merchants in London that had already been present in London for many years.[9] Therefore ›stranger church‹ is more appropriate than refugee church.

When Mary I (1516–1558) succeeded her brother as queen of England three years later, the protestant reformation was turned back. The leaders of the Dutch church fled to the continent, and via Denmark both the superintendent Jan Laski (1499–1560) and one of the ministers Marten Micron (1523–1559) ended up in Emden. There they published the forms and church order of the London Church, Laski the Latin *Forma ac ratio* (1555)[10] and Micron the Dutch *Christlicke Ordinancien*.[11] The books give an insight into the practical organization of the stranger

1568-1585, [Nieuwerkerk] 1994. The recent German study on Jan Laski's ecclesiology includes extensive chapters on the Dutch and Walloon stranger churches. Judith Becker, Gemeindeordnung und Kirchenzucht: Johannes a Lascos Kirchenordnung für London (1555) und die reformierte Konfessionsbildung, Studies in medieval and Reformation traditions, vol. 122, Leiden 2007, 259-537.

9 Pettegree estimates the number of adult male members of the Dutch and Walloon churches at about 700 in total in 1550 and about 1.400 in 1553. Pettegree, Foreign Protestant Communities, 77-78

10 This Form and Rationale was first published as Joannes a Lasco, Forma ac ratio tota ecclesiastici ministerij, in peregrinorum, potissimùm uerò Germanorum ecclesia: instituta Londini in Anglia, per pientissimum principem Angliæ &c. regem Edvardvm, eius nominis Sextu, [Frankfurt am Main] 1555. About the book cf. Becker, Gemeindeordnung und Kirchenzucht, 27-39 and Michael Stephen Springer, Restoring Christ's Church: John a Lasco and the Forma Ac Ratio, Aldershot 2007, 50-58. The work is included in Jan Laski, Joannis a Lasco Opera tam edita quam inedita, ed. A. Kuyper, Amsterdam 1866, vol. 2, 1-283.

11 Marten Micron, De christlicke ordinancien der Nederlantscher gemeynten Christi, die van den christelicken prince kon Edewaerdt den VI in het jaar 1550 te Londen ingesteld was, [Embden] 1554. A critical edition was edited by W.F. Dankbaar: Marten Micron, De christlicke ordinancien der Nederlantscher ghemeinten te Londen (1554), The Hague 1956.

church, at least as it should have functioned; the forms serve as a general model for other reformed churches.[12]

Marriage Form

In case of a marriage the names of the couple were announced three times in the congregation to avoid illegitimate relationships or the breaking of earlier promises. A promise before two or more witnesses was irrevocable.[13] Without this public announcement it was not even permitted for members of the Dutch Church to marry in the Church of England, a rule that led to several cases of church discipline.[14] The wedding ceremony took place on Sunday at the end of the morning service; bride and bridegroom were to attend the service without ›worldly pomp‹.[15] The warning seems to have been intended especially for the women, because it is repeated in the final admonition to the bride.[16]

The marriage form opens with the observation that married persons are generally subject to many anxieties and crosses. This may be a reference to the difficult situation of the refugees, but it is in the first place a polemical statement. Holy matrimony is despised by many, either by those who seek an easy life in lasciviousness or by those who seek a pretended holy life.[17] In other words, the hardships flowing from the

12 Springer, Restoring Christ's Church, 57 and Becker, Gemeindeordnung und Kirchenzucht, 37. The relationship between both publications is not completely clear, though Micron's Ordinancien seem to be the more original whereas Laski's Forma ac ratio the more complete text. Cf. the ›Vorwort‹ to the edition of the German text of Micron's Ordinancien, Marten Micron, Kirchenordnung, Heidelberg 1565, by Anneliese Spregler-Ruppenthal, Sehling, Emil ed., Die evangelischen Kirchenordnungen des 16. Jahrhunderts, vol. 7/II 1, Tübingen 1963, 552-667, 572.

13 Boersma, Vluchtig voorbeeld, 165.

14 Boersma, Vluchtig voorbeeld, 132.

15 ›De Bruydegom ende Bruyt ter ghesetter hueren, sonder eenighe wereltlicke pomperie, met alle tuchticheit (als den christenen betaemt) comen ter predicatie.‹ Micron, Christlicke ordinancien, 144.

16 Micron, Christlicke ordinancien, 144.

17 ›... so comt het, dat den heiighen huywelicken staet van velen in dese werelt veracht werdt, In sonderheit van allen den ghenen, die in onreinicheit een profytich ende ghemackelick, oft ooc een gheueinst heilich leuen soecken.‹ Micron, Christlicke ordinancien, 145. In the Canons of Trent those are condemned who say that the marriage state is to be placed above the state of

responsibilities of the relationship are no reason not to marry. The form even places monks and nuns living in celibacy on one level with fornicators.

The form encourages the couple to expect the help of God in all circumstances; marriage is good, because it is a divine institution. Next to the biblical references to Paradise and the wedding at Cana, the form also says that Christ, the Son of God, was willing to be born into a family; Josef and Mary were pledged to be married. Probably because of the seeming tension with Christ's virgin birth, the phrase was deleted from later editions of the form.[18]

Although not much attention is paid to affectionate love between spouses, it is remarkable that the first goal of marriage is not procreation, but mutual assistance of a husband and wife I all things. The second reason for marriage is to bring up children by instructing them in the true knowledge of God to his glory and the maintenance of the church. The third reason is to avoid sexual uncleanness and lead a pure and holy life.

In the admonition the bridegroom, as the head of his wife, is told to lead, educate, comfort, and defend her after Christ's example. With a reference to Ephesians 5, the form tells him to love his spouse as his own body. The bride is told to love, honor, and respect her husband and to be subject to him in all things as her Lord, like the church is subject to Christ. There is a strong emphasis on submissiveness. The early Protestants rejected ancient and medieval portrayals of women as physically, mentally, and morally inferior, but they insisted on the headship of the husband.[19]

The benediction illustrates that marriage should be characterized by mutual love and faithfulness: ›God almighty, who has called you to the marriage state bind you in the bond of true love that you may express in all your life the great hidden unity of Christ and his church.‹[20] The

virginity or of celibacy. Council of Trent, Canon 14, session 24. Denzinger-Schönmetzer, Enchiridion Symbolorum, 980.

18 ›Christus ooc, de sone Gods, heeft inden huywelicken staet willen gheboren syn‹ Micron, Christlicke ordinancien, 145. The phrase does not occur in the edition of the marriage form in the Psalm book (1566) of Petrus Dathenus (1531-1588) and accepted by the synod of Dordt (1618-1619).

19 Ozment, Ancestors, 36.

20 ›God almachtich die v tot den huywelicken staet gheropen heeft, binde v te samen met den bandt der warachtigher liefden: op dat ghy v gansche leuen de groote verborghen eenicheit Christi ende sijnder ghemeinten wtdrucken moecht. ‹ Micron, Christlicke ordinancien, 147.

closing prayer underlines this ›Bind them together in a faithful and true love. [...] Change the water of all their sorrows into the sweet wine of your comforts and grant them grace to live so godly together here, that they finally may be brought with us to eternal life, through Jesus Christ, your Son and our Lord. Amen.‹[21]

Christian Education

The church order deals with the Christian education of the baptized members. The stranger church in London had two catechisms, a larger catechism written by Laski and the *Cleyne Catechismus ojt Kinder Leere* by Micron.[22] The larger catechism consists of 250 questions and answers completely covering Christian doctrine and life. In the exposition of the fifth commandment it asks the children why they should honor their parents. They are to answer that it is reasonable to do so because ›they have brought us forth with pain and brought us up with great difficulty, care, and labor.‹[23]

The shorter catechism was used for the instruction of the baptized members of the church. The smaller children – from five years and upwards were examined on the first Sundays of March and September. They had to learn the Lord's Prayer, the Apostolic Creed and the Ten Commandments by heart. In a next phase of their education they had to memorize the shorter catechism. After the public examinations, the pastor admonished the parents to continue to educate their children in the fear of the Lord and thanked God that the mysteries of salvation were even revealed to the very young children of the congregation.[24] These two afternoon services replaced the normal services in which the larger catechism was recited by the oldest children and then explained by the minister. So in the Sunday afternoon services the young people

[21] ›Bindt'se te gader in een volstandighe en oprechte liefde. [...] Verandert het water aller haerer droeffenissen in eenen soeten wijn vwer troostingen: ende geeft haer ghenade, hier so Goddeick t'samen te lenen, dat sy ten einde met ons allen totten eewigen leuen ghebrocht moghen wesen: doer Jesnm Christum uwen Sone ende onsen Heere. Amen.‹ Micron, Christlicke ordinancien, 148.

[22] Marten Micron, De cleyne catechismus, oft kinder leere, der Duytscher ghemeynte, die te Londen is, London 1552. For the text cf. Johann Michael Reu, Quellen zur Geschichte des kirchlichen Unterrichts in der evangelischen Kirche Deutschlands zwischen 1530 und 1600, vol. I/3 2.3, Gütersloh 1924, 1149-1170.

[23] Laski, Opera 2, 376-377.

[24] Micron, Christlicke ordinancien, 67-68.

had a special place and twice a year the little children had their service, but never without first listening to a sermon for half an hour.

The form to accept the adolescents – as they are called by Laski[25] – to the communion table shows that this Christian education lasted until the children were almost fourteen, which was the age when many children would leave home either to study or to work. One week before a communion service, the new young members would be examined in front of the congregation, make confession of faith, and promise to remain faithful in their confession and submit to church discipline.

Although they were now accepted as full members, the parents were still held co-responsible for their spiritual life and are told not to give occasion for them to renounce their confession by being too lax.[26] If the teenagers reached the age of fourteen without making confession, the pastors had to inform why they were negligent. If the parents were to be blamed for the lack of knowledge or the ungodly life of their children, they were disciplined for the ›unutterably great sin‹ of failing in the Christian education.[27] If only the children were guilty, the parents were comforted and counseled how to deal with their obstinate children. In the meantime the pastors would speak to them from the word of God, firmly – yet with wisdom – presenting to them Gods punishments. At the age of eighteen or twenty baptized members could be excommunicated as despisers of the grace and covenant of God. Baptism does not make someone a Christian without a Christian life.[28] In practice this form of church discipline probably was seldom; the minutes of the London consistory are rather silent on the issue.

25 Laski, Opera 2, 98-100.

26 ›D]e Dienaer vermaent de Ouders tot een stedighe sorghe totten kinderen: op dat sy doer haerder slappicheit niet veruallen van het ghene dat sy beleden hebben.‹ Micron, Christlicke ordinancien, 70.

27 ›Daer na ist dat sy de vermaninghen verachten: so werden sy van dese groote onwtsprekelicke sonde ghestraft, nae de ordene ende heysch der christeicker straffen.‹ Micron, Christlicke ordinancien, 70.

28 ›dat het niet ghenouchsaem sy om een christen te syne, dat wy den seghel des verbonts, namelick den Doop, in ons kintschap ontfanghen hebben, ende ons also met den naeme Christi tot synder oneere vercieren, ten sy dat ons leuen daer nae metten seluen ouer een come.‹ Micron, Christlicke ordinancien, 71.

No minutes have survived from the short Edwardian period of the London Church; they are all from a later period; the church order and liturgy from that first period, however, remained fundamental for the ecclesiastical practice in the Dutch Church. In 1559, following the coronation of Elisabeth I (1533-1603), refugees started to return to London. In 1560 the church was reinstituted, although it lost its autonomy and was subject to the bishop of London. The extensive minutes of the consistory, the so-called *Kerkeraads-Protokollen* from 1560–1563 and from 1569–1585 have been published.[29] These minutes offer some insight into family life.

There are more cases of church discipline on marriage than on the education of children, but there are a few useful references. One Sebastiaen Pieterssen, a schoolmaster, is accused by a father that he has treated his child so unreasonably that it became ill. It is not clear whether it is a boy or a girl or how old the child is. It might have been a student from the school or a young servant. The father is asked to find witnesses and the schoolmaster is summoned before the consistory. One of the witnesses says that she has seen Sebastiaens wife putting the child in cold water and then beating it severely. Sebastiaen, however, denies that his wife did anything else than washing the child and declares that the child was healthy on going home. The consistory tells him to reconcile himself with the father. At least the father has some parental affection and, moreover the consistory deemed the case severe enough to investigate.[30]

Some cases of ill-treatment of maid-servants are reported in the minutes.[31] Adrian Henricks and his wife are accused of flogging their fifteen year old maid because she did not wake up at four or five in the morning, while they had kept her busy until eleven at night the day before.[32] There are also cases of sexual abuse. An older man is accused of raping a girl of eleven or twelve years old. After being in prison for some

[29] Aart A. van Schelven, Kerkeraads-protocollen der Nederduitsche Vluchtelingen-Kerk te Londen 1560-1563, Amsterdam 1921, and Auke Jelsma and Owe Boersma, Acta van het Consistorie van de Nederlandse gemeente te Londen: 1569-1585, The Hague 1993.

[30] Jelsma and Boersma, Acta, 169-172 (entries 564, 566, 574).

[31] Jelsma and Boersma, Acta, 209-210 (entries 704, 712).

[32] Jelsma and Boersma, Acta, 453-454, 457, 460-461 (entries 1986-1990, 2006, 2019, 2027).

months – a short period according to modern standards – he confesses his sins before the congregation.[33] In all cases of ill-treatment of children the consistory – after hearing the person who is accused – acknowledges the charges of family or neighbors and supports the child.[34]

Sometimes the consistory felt responsible to warn parents for not treating their children well enough. One mother is warned for not giving his son what he needed – perhaps she refused him food and drink – she replied that she wanted to punish him because he was behaving so badly. She is admonished and warned that the elders would ask for more information and summon her again if necessary. Apparently her husband toke offence, for the next week he visited the consistory with her to ask who had accused her. The consistory replied that is was not an official charge but only a warning.[35]

Marriage

Many entries in the minutes regard the marriage relationship. It is difficult to draw conclusions about affectionate love from a number of cases of adultery and fornication, but reading in between lines, one can conclude what was felt as a normal Christian behavior.

In august 1583 the consistory receives a report that the widow Heylken Karmans is spreading the rumor that she has slept with Phillips Crespeel on the condition that she would marry him. Summoned before the elders she tells her story. After dating with Phillips he brought her back home and asked her if she would marry him. She consented and he said that he had promised himself never to marry anyone without first sleeping with her. Then he forced her to sexual intercourse. Phillips however denied the whole thing and was believed by the consistory.[36] When Heylken wanted to attend the Lord's Supper again, after a year and a half, she had to admit that she had falsely accused Phillips, which of course does not mean that it certainly was not true. In this case the

33 Jan Coene alias De Grave finally admits the abuse. Jelsma and Boersma, Acta, 645-646, 662-663, 669, 676 (entries 2952, 2957-2958, 3042-3044, 3065, 3099). Hans Waldkneel is accused of sexual abuse of two boys of eleven and thirteen. Jelsma and Boersma, Acta, 613 (entry 2745).

34 Boersma, Vluchtig voorbeeld, 142.

35 Jelsma and Boersma, Acta, 202 (entries 675, 680).

36 Jelsma and Boersma, Acta, 669-671, 754 (entries 3064, 3068-3072, 3501) Sexual contact as part of the engagement was usual but prohibited in the reformed church.

suspicion might have been due to the fact that she was notorious in the consistory for an offensive life and drunkenness. In general, men and women were treated equally in church discipline. If a woman accused a man of a sexual offense, the case was seriously investigated and if a woman declared being with child from a certain man, he had to prove the opposite, which was not easy in most cases.[37]

After a rumor that Zeger van Scherburg and his wife were drunk, both are told not to partake of the Lord's Supper. The elders investigate the case and witnesses report that Zeger is away from home or working downstairs in his shop, while some other man is with his wife Lynken upstairs from ten in the morning until six at night, to the offense of the landlord and neighbors. A female witness accuses Zeger himself of indecent proposals. [38] Two weeks later Zeger furiously denies the accusations before the consistory and tells the elders that his neighbors are gossiping.[39] Two months later, Andries, a former servant, witnesses, that about one year ago Lynken came home completely drunk at midnight together with the English maid. Zeger also came home late at night several times with a maid. Once he was angry that Andries was not sleeping yet. Three hours later Zeger and the maid were still together. Andries tells the consistory that he warned his boss about his behavior, but was beaten.

A young girl stays the night with the couple and is surprised that they do not sleep together. Lynken tells her that this because of her toothache. She sleeps with Lynken, but wakes up at six in the morning because a stranger is standing next to the bed asking Lynken who the girl is. A female member of the church tells the consistory that Zeger visited her and did not go home in the evening, but wanted to sleep with her, because her husband was not at home. After admonishing him that this was unchristian behavior, he replied: »My wife has given me consent to do anything I want, as long as she does not know about it.«[40] Zeger kept denying, but the elders found the evidence convincing enough to announce his name publicly.

Short stories like these show that families of Dutch strangers in London were rather open because of the presence of servants in the family. A widow living with two young men is summoned to let them move. In stead she marries one of them, who is not a member of the

37 Becker, Gemeindeordnung und Kirchenzucht, 217 n395.
38 Jelsma and Boersma, Acta, 339-340 (entry 1382).
39 Jelsma and Boersma, Acta, 349 (entry 1426).
40 Jelsma and Boersma, Acta, 367 (entry 1503).

church. A few months later she is seen staying the night over with a physician after drinking with him.[41] A son of a well-known family turns out to have married one of the maids secretly against the will of his family when they still lived in Antwerp. She complains to the consistory that he and his family do not want to acknowledge the relationship.[42]

One couple, named Aernout de Keysere and Eyken van Erckendale, had been living as husband and wife for some time already; he was renting a room from a widow and she was the maid. After moving to London the widowed dies and the couple wants to marry. The consistory agrees after confession of sin but asks the former congregation if there was no hindrance. Then it turns out that Eyken has been married before in 's-Hertogenbosch. She claims that her former husband has died in Brussels, but can not sufficiently prove that. In the meantime the couple marries in the Church of England, but the Dutch consistory decides that they have to divorce until it is clear that Eyken's first husband is dead. Finally Aernout decides to travel to Brussels himself, after which nothing is heard of him anymore, at least not in the minutes.[43]

5 Conclusions

The church order, liturgy and consistory minutes show that there was love and affection in early modern family relationships, or at least that the refugees and other strangers agreed that there ought to be love and affection in the family. The care for Christian education in the several stages of the development of the baptized members and the firm resistance of cases of ill-treatment show that – though times and culture were different – childhood did exist in the early modern period. The aim of church discipline was to keep the body of Christ pure and holy. The system seems to have functioned, but it seems rather difficult for the consistory to keep an eye on the godly walk of the members in the metropolitan context of early modern London. Next to quantitative evidence from public records and qualitative information from family archives the consistory minutes offer a source of information on the early modern family that is more personal than the records and still less subjective than most ego-documents.

41 Jelsma and Boersma, Acta, 148 (entry 486).

42 Jelsma and Boersma, Acta, 593-597 (entries 2634-2655).

43 Jelsma and Boersma, Acta, 42-43, 62-63, 70-73, 85, 92, 95 (entries 134, 138, 201, 225, 229, 270, 298, 309).

The most striking difference between the early modern and the modern families is that at the time of the Reformation the nuclear family was surrounded by male and female servants that lived with the family and influenced the relationships.[44] It is surprising that the official liturgical forms remain silent on this so important issue. In many, if not most, of the problems in family-relationships the members of group play a significant role, either as victims, offenders, or as witnesses. This might have been strengthened by the fact that the families were uprooted from their original homeland and lacked the original context of the extended families. However, whether the specific situation of the members of a refugee or stranger church made any difference in this respect, can not be concluded without comparing the material to non-stranger situations.

Secular historiography has often blamed confessional historiography of being biased and not always without cause. Too often, history has only been studied to find a norm for today. Secular historians, however, can also be biased, by taking the present as a norm for interpreting history. Resent research on family life shows that notwithstanding many differences, there is a line of continuity. Or to quote Steven Ozment: ›For a modern age faced with family crisis, there is good news from the recovered history of the family: this smallest and seemingly most fragile of institutions (is) proving itself to be humankind's bedrock as well as it's fault line.‹[45]

44 MacCulloch, Reformation, 617.
45 Ozment, Ancestors, 111-112.

Extended Family as a *familia Dei*

A Small Family Picture

Maarten Kater

1 Introduction

Why cannot the Church restrict and initially approach the family as the *familia Dei*?[1] This is the question presently posed for discussion. Using systematic theology, we will reflect on the empirical forms of family life, a human form of kinship.

Joint reflection and debate on the topic of the *familia Dei* is a matter of *inter-esse.* Hannah Arendt's work on ›zwischenmenschlicher Sozialität‹ (interhuman sociality) as the hallmark of human life is an example.[2] But what is contained in the ›inter‹, the ›between‹ between two ›beings‹ (*esse*)? An obstacle here would result in nothing getting across. A common example would be the huge difference between a face-to-face family meeting in mutual love, and a one-to-many oration delivered from behind a wooden lectern.

This *inter-esse* matters to the extended family, though not just as an ›inter-esse‹, an interrelationship *within* mankind. This relates to

1 Cf. *Confessio Belgica*, art. 35 ›We believe and confess that our Savior Jesus Christ did ordain and institute the sacrament of the Holy Supper to nourish and support those whom He has already regenerated and incorporated in *his family, which is his church*‹. Not to mention the unique position within the *familia Dei* of the people of Israel!

2 Cf. Burkhard Liersch, ›Einleitung‹, in: idem (Hrsg.), Sozialphilosophie, Freiburg 1999, 23-24.

theology first- and foremost, and is not merely a matter of sociological anthropology. Rebekka A. Klein recently proposed that a contribution of *theological* anthropology to an interdisciplinary dialogue on the *sociality of human nature* would be useful. She argued the view that theology should not employ the biological difference of man and animal to reflect on social humanity, instead focusing on the ethical ambivalence of social humanity and inhumanity in an interdisciplinary dialogue with the social sciences. This means theology should conceptualize a phenomenology of interpersonal relations, which faces the possible neglect of inhumanity and offers a grammar of sociality, explicating the difference between humanity and inhumanity using the perspective of *coram Deo*.[3]

What kinship and which relations do we have in mind when referring to the *familia Dei* from a point of view, which does not start with the Church as the *familia Dei*? What does the word ›extended‹ entail? Extended from which starting-point, that of a *pater familias*? Extended to which horizon, that of all humanity? This last suggestion is logically possible, as the concept of good neighbourship is at the heart of the *familia Dei.* Well, using good neighbourship as a starting point one is able to draw up an ›extended family‹ tree in the following way. If *A* is to be a good neighbour to all the people he knows, each of those are to be good neighbours to all the people they know, some of which will fall outside the group first mentioned, and so forth.

Quite a few questions have been raised up to this point. Only a few answers will be given in our exploration of some reasons to look at humanity as a *familia Dei* in our systematic theological reflections and considerations.

I will reflect on the extended family as a *familia Dei* from the perspectives of:

Firstly, the ›womb‹ of this kinship.

Secondly, the ›tomb‹ of this kinship.

1 The ›womb‹ of this kinship

›In the beginning‹ (Gen 1:1; John 1:1) there was neither *pater familias* nor Church, but only the *Pater Filii*: ›In the beginning was the Word,

[3] Rebekka A. Klein, ›Die Inhumanität des Animal Sociale. Vier Thesen zum interdisziplinären Beitrag der theologischen Anthropologie‹, NZSTh 51, 2009, 427-444.

and the Word was with (*pros*) God, and the Word was God‹ (John 1:1). In the beginning was God, *this* God and Father; the Father of the Son, Jesus Christ. He is the Son who is at Father's side as the one-of-a-kind Son *(monogenes)*, as God in his own right (John 1:18). Therefore, I would like to suggest that in reflecting on the extended family as *familia Dei* in a Trinitarian theology, one is to start with this unity: ›God as communion‹. The communion of this unique divine *familia Dei* exists in three persons, the Father, the Son, and the Holy Spirit. In the beginning there was a fullness of life and love between the Father, the Son and the Holy Spirit. Thus, in a special, very unique sense the communion between the Father, the Son, and the Spirit constitutes the One ›*Familia Dei*‹. To characterize these special ›family relations‹, consider the πρός from John 1:1, ὁ λόγος ἦν πρός τὸν Θεον. Here πρός not only establishes a relationship between God and the Word, but it simultaneously *distinguishes* the two[4], which could denote *otherness-in-relation.* This is a pattern which takes a central place in the trinitarian theology of Colin E. Gunton.[5]

So does ›extended family‹ suggest family life is like an extension of God? Does Paul's sermon on Mars hill point to such a relation between Creator and creation when he said, ›For we are indeed his offspring‹ (Acts 17: 29)? To phrase the question differently: does the extended family of the human race relate to God, the Triune God as a ›*familia Dei*‹, by way of an extension of God?

In biblical teaching there is an absolute ontological distinction between Creator and creation. Gunton states in a definition of Christian

4 Cf. the use of παρά (+ genetive or dative) in the Gospel of John. For a balanced overview of πρός: M.J. Harris, NIDNTT, Vol.3, 1204-7. Cf. Andreas J. Köstenberger, John [BECNT], Grand Rapids 2004, 27.

5 Particularly consult Colin E. Gunton, ›Trinity, Ontology and Anthropology: Towards a Renewal of the Doctrine of the *Imago Dei*‹, in: Christoph Schwöbel, Colin E. Gunton, Persons, Divine and Human, Edingburgh 1999, 1991, 47-61, 59: ›To be a person is to be constituted in particularity and freedom – to be given space to be – by others in community. *Otherness* and *relation* continue to be the two central and polar concepts here.‹ This is mentioned by Gunton in relation with ›Space to be Human: the Trinity‹. Cf. Gunton, Act and Being, 121: ›If the Son and the Spirit are in different ways focuses of God's movement outwards, to the other, God's aseity, the doctrine of his ontological integrity and completeness, will serve as the basis (...) of the creation's integrity, as truly itself by virtue of its being created in the Son and by the power of the Spirit‹; Gunton, The Promise of Trinitarian Theology, London/New York 2003, 1997², 14: ›[I]t is argued that the doctrine of the Trinity enables us to think both the otherness (...) from God, and the relatedness of the world to God‹.

ontology that »there are no degrees of being but two realities, God and everything else that he has made, the created order.«[6] These two absolute, distinct realities nevertheless became related ›in Christ‹ when our Creator made heaven and earth. However, this relation could once again be characterized by an *otherness-in-relation,* which is typical also for family life as a given fact and as a gift. It is this special family relation in which creatures come into being, even though they do not necessarily experience the ties of family life.

By creating men and women as a part of ›all things‹ ›in Christ‹ (Col. 1:16), the Triune God grants them the privilege of being a part of an extended family as a *familia Dei*. The preposition ›in‹ when used in the clause ›in Christ‹ is not merely instrumental or local from a grammatical perspective, but rather has a relational dimension. Therefore family life and humanity as an extended *familia Dei* have some family traits. We should emphasize the concept of the *imago Dei* here. ›Then God said: ›Let us make humankind in our image, according to our likeness‹ (Gen 1:26). Semantically the word ›likeness‹ has many shades of meaning, ranging from a vague similitude to an exact copy or blueprint.[7] In any case, humankind, both male and female, was to reflect its Father as the man created in *the* image of God, the Son:

Keeping in mind the relational dimensions of the *imago Dei* and the decisive archetypal function of the eternal Son, what is more natural than defining the created being's relation to his Creator in Father – son language? As children created in God's image, men and women are shaped by an ability, which is beyond that of other creatures: the ability to relate profoundly to one another and to their Father and Creator. The description of the original intimacy Adam and Eve enjoyed with the Creator is notably familiar, and even *familial* in nature (cf. Gen 3:8).[8]

6 Gunton, The Triune Creator, Grand Rapids/Cambridge 1998, 54 (cf. 36, 39, 81).

7 Modern exegetes generally agree, largely on the basis of Hebrew parallelism, that the terms ›likeness‹ and ›image‹ are virtually synonymous.

8 David B. Garner, ›The First and Last Son: Christology and Sonship in Pauline Soteriology‹, in: Lane G. Tipton, Jeffrey C. Waddington (eds.), Resurrection and Eschatology, Phillipsburg 2008, 255-279, 268; cf. Karl Barth for his exposition of human relationality, Church Dogmatics III:4 (in connection with CD III:1, esp. par. 41).

We will now sum up these remarks concerning the relational make-up of humanity[9] as a part of the *imago Dei* concept. We view the human race as a whole as the largest extended family. The ›womb‹ of kinship within this human race is the love and the life of the Triune God. It is the bond of life and love in which He created mankind by his Spirit ›in Christ‹.

2 *The ›tomb‹ of kinship*

It is a pity that this sphere of *inter-esse* has been filled and obstructed by the *ego*. Sin caused mutual love to change into self-love: *homo incurvatus in se.* The reality of *homo homini lupus* entered into the world. What does being a part of the same extended family mean when one member of the *familia Dei* murders another, when his question ›am I my brother's keeper? ‹ (Gen 4:9) becomes the song of mankind? Whether or how the image of God is lost is a complex issue indeed. At this point, a few remarks on this broad subject are appropriate. Sin caused a clean break with our Creator. Has this break distorted all family life? Did the extended family wither and shrink into a lonely ego?

In reference to the *imago Dei,* Alistair McFadyen makes the distinction between ›a permanent and indestructible structure‹ at the ontological level and ›the concrete conditions of human communication overbearingly distorted‹ at a practical level.[10] Does this distinction hold? I think it does not. The human race is certainly still called to account as being created in the *imago Dei* (e.g. Gen 9:6). This means one has the calling to be and behave as a member of the extended family. Love has however been changed into enmity between members of the same family. Kinship on the ontological level still exists: sin has no right to exist. However, the members of the family are ›dead through the trespasses and sins‹ (Eph 2:1). The ›tomb‹ of kinship has been filled with love. Love, the love to God and our neighbour, has been buried.

9 Cf. Marcel Sarot, ›Trinity and Church: Trinitarian Perspectives on the Identity of Christian Community‹, IJST 12, 2010, 33-45, 37: ›God's relationship with human beings is not a relationship with individuals, but with a community. (...) The relationship between God and humanity is not a relationship between two individuals, then, but a relationship between a community and a Trinity: the triune God.‹

10 Alistair McFadyen, The Call to Personhood: A Christian Theory of the Individual in Social Relationships, Cambridge 1990, 39-43.

The fall from intimacy with the Creator required banishment from his holy presence in Eden (Gen 3:23–24). The intimacy once shared is now compromised. The precious closeness man enjoyed with his Creator as a Father became a disastrous segregation. As a consequence, he was also segregated from his fellow humans. In God's image man enjoyed a relationship with the Creator and the creation in a *familial* fashion. Under the curse of sin, *a relational reality exists* only in the sense of a *banished* remoteness.[11]

However, the ›tomb‹ of kinship is empty, for Jesus Christ lives forever! ›In Him‹ man lives *coram Deo* in his *imago Dei*. The kinship that matters portrays to us the extended family as a *familia Dei* (Mark 3:31–34). The *familia Dei* ultimately is the eschatological reality when ›God may be all in all‹ (1 Cor 15:28).[12]

I suggest that, from the viewpoint of the extended family as a *familia Dei*, the following points are of particular interest for further theological reflection:

1. To be a person is to be constituted in *particularity* and *freedom* to others in *community* (*familia*); the co-presence of both (*otherness* and *relation*) will rule out both egalitarianism and forms of individualism. Both egalitarianism and individualism belong to the ›tomb of kinship‹. There is no ›womb of kinship‹ without ›otherness-in-relation‹.

2. The disorientation and disintegration of sin lead to separation, alienation, segmentation and finally to destruction within the extended family as a *familia Dei*.

3. There is no separation of *created sociality* and *redeemed sociality*, because they are related in Christ by *otherness-in-relation*, even though the extended family as a *familia Dei* is an eschatological reality brought into existence by the Spirit of Christ.

4. To connect the Triune God to the extended family as *familia Dei* is not to copy the life of the Triune God in the life of this family as a mirror-structure. After all, humankind in the *imago Dei* is to be

11 David B. Garner, ›The First and Last Son‹, 268.

12 Cf. Christoph Schwöbel, ›Human Being As Relational Being: Twelve Theses for a Christian Anthropology‹, in: Christoph Schwöbel, Colin E. Gunton, Persons, Divine and Human, 141-170, 165: ›*The community of faith in the church is the anticipation of and witness to the perfect fulfilment of the fellowship of the triune God with his reconciled creation in the Kingdom of God*‹ (12th Thesis).

characterized as *otherness*-in-relation. Only one exact copy has been shown and given: the Son as the *imago Dei* (Hebr 1:3).

Homosexuality: Improving the Traditional Theory?

Ad de Bruijne

1 Introduction

Today neither churches nor Christians can allow themselves to neglect reflection on homosexuality. Even smaller orthodox communities in the Western world now struggle to find clarity of vision and practical direction in this regard. Other parts of the world church probably sooner or later will follow. As an ethicist in one of the smaller Reformed churches in the Netherlands I almost weekly feel the urgency of the questions.

The present paper tries to achieve two aims. First, it attempts to reconsider the traditional orthodox view on homosexuality. A scientific theological attitude should not repeat its certainties but rather should face remaining questions and challenges. Secondly, and in so doing, I invite the contrary position in the same-sex debate to do the same. While some certainties of the modernists challenge the traditionalists, their certainties could in turn stimulate some critical self-evaluation amongst these modernists.

As a first step I sketch a traditional view on homosexuality. After that I select some problems within this theory that remain unsolved. This then leads to an effort to improve the theory and an invitation to adherents of alternative positions to enter into a renewed dialogue.

The classic Protestant position on homosexuality consists of three dimensions.[1] In the first place, one finds a Divine Command ethics in which exegetical results are used straightforwardly to condemn homosexual intercourse. Secondly, one finds an element of natural law ethics in which a conviction about natural creation ordinances offers an interpretative context for this biblical condemnation. In the third place is a salvation historical model that explains the existence of something like a homosexual identity. This counts not as sinful itself but as one of the consequences and disturbances with which sin affected the originally good creation.

For some time this classic orthodox position was judged to be untenable. Many theologians and other Christians today still echo this judgement. Yet, recently the orthodox position has made a comeback. Influences from other parts of the world-church, the revival of evangelicalism and a growing suspicion of the more radical bible criticism have contributed to that. In particular, the exegetical dimension in this traditional theory has proved stronger than ever. The moderate biblical scholar Robert Gagnon, for example, has built a convincing traditional case, though he unfortunately evinces a degree of homophobia.[2]

Gagnon proves from Ancient Near Eastern texts that the Biblical prohibition of homosexual intercourse cannot be relativized as only contextual. Nor is it possible to explain the biblical words at stake as limited to a cultic scope, to heterosexual perversions or to unequal relations. He also uncovers a consistent line of thought in Old and New Testament and in extra-biblical Jewish literature. This line of thought originates in the creation story about the polarity of man and woman and proves to be the foremost background of biblical passages condemning homosexual intercourse. Like Richard Hays[3] and others, Gagnon takes

1 J. Douma, Homofilie, Kampen 1984; idem, The Ten Commandments: Manual for the Christian Life, Phillipsburg 1996; Jürgen-Burkhardt Klautke, Gegen die Schöpfung: Homosexualität im Licht der Heiligen Schrift, Neuhofen 1998; John M. Frame, The Doctrine of Christian Life, Philipsburg 2008.

2 Robert A.J. Gagnon, The Bible and homosexual Practices: Texts and Hermeneutics, Nashville 2001.

3 Richard B. Hays, The Moral Vision of the New Testament: Community, Cross, new Creation, a contemporary Introduction to the New Testament Ethics, Edinburgh 1997.

the ›giving up‹ of natural intercourse in Romans 1 not as indicating a decision in personal biographies but as denoting a collective transition in human history. Humanity suppressed the knowledge of the Creator and now experiences the consequences in growing accustomed to what contradicts the structures of creation. Gagnon, amongst others, has also show that stable and equal homosexual relations were not unknown in antiquity. He even claims that the ancients sensed something like a concept of homosexual identity. Gagnons opponents often feel no need to contradict his results. Gagnon himself uses an exegete like Bernadette Brooten, who advocates gay love and yet concludes that Paul leaves no room for that. In response, she feels no obligation to obey Paul's voice.[4]

3 Challenges

We now proceed to the second step. This traditional position confronts at least five challenges.

3.1 Reality and character

The first challenge concerns ethical theory. The traditional approach is a version of a Divine Command Ethics. Moral rules are considered to be decisive. However, even orthodox ethicists today think such an approach, at the very least, to be one-sided.[5] It amounts to a Christianized version of Kant's foundationalist ethics. It lacks for example a utilitarian moment. What is one to do with the empirical fact that many orthodox homosexuals cannot uphold the life that suits this theory and not infrequently end up in sexual disorder or leave their churches? Does having a firm view on homosexuality outweigh the departure of homosexuals themselves?

4 Bernadette Brooten, Love Between Women: Early Christian Responses to Female Homoeroticism, Chicago 1996; Mark D. Smith, ›Ancient Bisexuality and the Interpretation of Romans 1:26-27‹ in: Journal of the American Academy of Religion LXIV/2, Oxford 1996; Dan O. Via, in: Dan O. Via; Robert A.J. Gagnon, Homosexuality and the Bible: Two Views, Minneapolis 2003.

5 Patrick Nullens, Verlangen naar het goede: bouwstenen voor een christelijke ethiek, Zoetermeer 2006; Patrick Nullens, Ronald T. Michener, The Matrix of Christian Ethics: Integrating Philosophy and Moral Theology in a Postmodern Context, Colorado Springs (USA)/Secunderabad (India) 2010.

Moral rules, moreover, should function within the context of reality. The usual static natural law model of creation ordinances is not sufficient. The Bible pictures a continuing history with its climax in the coming of God's kingdom. Such a model allows for change and development. When the kingdom approaches, marriage and family will be transformed into new forms of community, and perhaps also sexuality will undergo such a transformation.[6]

Moral rules, additionally, ask for a context of character. An ethics of conduct remains ineffective without acknowledging the role of virtue, moral formation and embodied community narrative. The primary ethical task does not consist of achieving theoretical moral conclusions but of following Jesus and mirroring the beauty and glory of God. Ethical conclusions demand a context of exemplary Christians who embody a convincing and attractive way of life that reflects the gospel. This alone could change the deterring effects of orthodox theory on many homosexuals.

3.2 Remaining differences

The second challenge is hermeneutical. Although homosexuality, as it is found in the world around the Bible, proved much more similar to the contemporary phenomenon than many christians today think, this should not eclipse our honest evaluation of remaining differences. These could change even the traditional moral position. Despite Gagnon and others, I see at least four remaining differences:

1. Nowhere does the Bible speak about homosexuality as a practical pastoral problem within the community of the church. Rather, it counts homosexuality as something typically pagan that after conversion is left behind. So, the most urgent situation of today seems to be absent from the Bible. Where does it refer to Christian boys or girls who against their will discover their homosexual preference? How can they recognize themselves in what the Bible pictures as typical mark of a pagan society that denies its Creator?
2. The modern concept of identity remains unique, even if we grant that in antiquity homosexuality could sometimes perhaps be seen as

6 Ad de Bruijne, ›De neocalvinistische politieke traditie en het gezinsbeleid van 2008, in: Gerrit de Kruijf; Petruschka Schaafsma (red.), Meer dan een optelsom: kanttekeningen bij de waarde van het gezin, Kampen 2008.

innate. Notions like individual subjectivity, introspective self-consciousness and authentic self-expression are typically modern.[7] In antiquity individual life was guided by fixed frame-works and roles. Not being able to live out your identity today causes severe inner conflicts and is experienced as more difficult than in biblical times.

3. Today, not being able to enter into a personal love relation creates a heavier burden than in biblical times. In antiquity either the household or the Christian congregation functioned as families in which individual life remained embedded. Modern individualism without such surrounding communities gives affective relations a particularly urgent character. The 19th century romantic ideals of emotional fulfilment in marriage and in the nuclear family strengthen the feeling that living without such relations is unbearable.
4. Sexuality no longer counts as functional or even as a power to control before it can be enjoyed. It has become an indispensable basic human need. Like eating, drinking, and leisure, moreover, it was incorporated in a consumerist way of life. Living without sexual fulfilment is considered to be unnatural and almost impossible.

3.3 Sub-stories

A third challenge results from the postmodern deconstruction of modern sexual morality[8]. Beneath the surface of the official narrative, sub-stories were detected. The sub-story of a dominant male culture that considers homosexuality to be a threat, is one example, another is the sub-story of romantic love between man and wife in civil marriage that marginalizes the concept of singleness. Classical positions, telling stories of natural law or Divine Commands cannot escape the question of whether their presumed universal principles perhaps also contain such hidden sub-stories.

[7] Charles Taylor, A Secular Age, Cambridge, MA 2007; Dale S. Kuehne, Sex and the World: Rethinking Relationship beyond an Age of Individualism, Grand Rapids 2009.

[8] Michel Foucault, The History of Sexuality: volumes 1, 2, 3 (An Introduction; The Use of Pleasure; The Care of self), New York 1990; Jonathan Dollimore, Sexual Dissidence: Augustine to Wilde, Freud to Foucault, Oxford 1991.

3.5 Open to compromise

The fourth challenge points to the possibility of compromises as acknowledged in most forms of orthodox ethics, for example in cases of divorce and remarriage. Following Calvin, they often practise equity and mildness, while at the same time upholding their principles.[9] Why then do many traditional churches hesitate to demonstrate such equity with respect to homosexuality? Could this reveal a homophobic sub-story? What would a compromise on this item possibly look like?

3.6 Biblical accommodation

The fifth challenge asks whether perhaps biblical moral conclusions about homosexuality should be corrected from the perspective of present-day experience. Even orthodox Christians allow for moments of accommodation in God's revelation.[10] He apparently did not correct all inadequate visions about illness, world-view, violence, slavery, and women. Could we detect also in the biblical words about homosexuality such accommodation to an existing horizon of knowledge? In the present day, biology, psychiatry, social science and genetics produce theories about homosexuality. For some the wide-spread existence of homosexuality among animals suggests that it is not an anomaly but an evolutionary possibility. Should modern experience and scientific results stimulate us to abandon biblical evaluations as outdated?

4 Improving the existing theory

A theory, which cannot solve its remaining problems, will, in the end, be abandoned. However, a sincere effort should first be made to improve the theory. In my opinion, this is indeed possible: there is no need for its abandonment.

Decisive in reaching this assertion is the conviction that the last and strongest challenge should be refuted. In orthodox Reformed theology

[9] Guenther H. Haas, The Concept of Equity in Calvin's Ethics, Carlisle 1997; J. Douma, Grondslagen: christelijke ethiek, Kampen 1999; idem, Responsible Conduct: Principle of Christian Ethics, Phillipsburg 2003.

[10] B. Loonstra, De geloofwaardigheid van de bijbel, Zoetermeer 1994; idem, Zo goed en zo kwaad: naar een ethiek van de christelijke gemeente, Zoetermeer 2000.

we have to set boundaries for the concept of accommodation. As soon as this would affect central elements of the biblical narrative, it would contradict the faith in revelation. Apparently, God sometimes did and sometimes did not surpass contextual limitations. To distinguish between both we should examine the communicative intent of texts, the measure in which words were counter-cultural and their relation to the overall biblical narrative.[11]

In many respects biblical words about homosexual intercourse indeed were counter-cultural. Besides, for example in Romans they are at the heart of Paul's communicative intent. In addition to this, we find them on some highways through biblical narrative, like the creation of man and woman, the image of God, the covenant between God and Israel, the unity between Christ and his church and the consummation of all relationships in the eschatological community. Therefore I consider their explanation as accomodations to be unjustified.

Nor could it be maintained that scientific results urge us to do so. It still seems possible not to treat the homosexual preference as a variant like a different colour of the eyes but as a disturbance, like a kind of handicap. Developmental psychology *and* modern gender theory both suggest that someone's life story also contributes to the emergence or even construction of a homosexual identity. And an appeal to animal homosexuality easily leads into a reverse version of the classic naturalistic fallacy. Facts from nature as such cannot be treated as moral guidelines.

That said, improvements to the existing theory are urgently needed.

In the first place the hidden influence of homophobic sub-stories must be deconstructed. This would result in more balance between the energy spent on this moral item and on others. There is little reason that homosexuality should take more of our attention than poverty, environment, media, justice and others. Homosexual intercourse as presumed moral failure concerns far less people than the other failures, while at the same time contrary to these it does no harm to others. Only if it would depart from the fixation on this problem, the traditional theory could regain credibility.

11 Kevin J. Vanhoozer, The Drama of Doctrine: a Canonical-Linguistic Approach to Christian Theology, Louisville 2005; idem (ed.), Everyday Theology: How to read Cultural Texts and interpret Trends, Grand Rapids 2007; William J. Webb, Slaves, Women & Homosexuals: exploring the Hermeneutics of Cultural Analysis, Downers Grove 2001.

This secondly leads to a greater openness to consider compromises. A possible compromise would be to prefer a stable sexual relationship between two partners to what sometimes turns out to be the only alternative, namely promiscuity. If traditional ethics accepts all kinds of compromises on other questions, it would be wrong to dismiss this compromise out of hand, as it is often the case. Yet, personally I remain reluctant to accept such a compromise, perhaps running the risk of unnoticed homophobic undertones. I see a real problem with it, not so much for the church but for homosexuals themselves. A compromise in this form would burden them with a repeated conflict of conscience. If homosexual intercourse counts as sin, it has to be confessed. But can we deliberately repeat what we have confessed? In this respect the compromise of accepting remarriage after unjustified divorce is different. There, the wrong decision itself takes place only once.

My thoughts on possible compromises take another direction. With the Anglican ethicist Oliver O'Donovan I am inclined to interpret a homosexual relationship not in terms of the marriage bond between man and wife but as a special possibility of friendship.[12] Within friendship forms of affection and even bodily intimacy are possible, more than in our Western culture is practised. Biblical prohibition is restricted to homosexual intercourse, and does not cover every kind of intimacy between members of the same gender. Homosexuals often possess specific gifts of sensitivity, nearness and friendship with which they confront the lack of affectivity and the poor concept of friendship in the traditionally male dominated societies of the Western world.[13] They could enrich and correct one-sided images of male and female identity and relationships. Here, the orthodox position should take a further step within its salvation historical theological framework. Because of this framework, today most adherents of the traditional position accept the existence of something like a homosexual identity as a given since the fall. Building on that vision, they should acknowledge the fact that in

12 Oliver O'Donovan, ›Homosexuality in the Church: Can there be a fruitful theological debate?‹ in: Timothy Bradshaw (ed.), The Way Forward? Christian Voices on Homosexuality and the Church, Grand Rapids 1997 (2-2003); idem, A Conversation Waiting to begin; The Churches and the Gay Controversy, Norwich 2009; about the concept of friendship e.g. E.D.H. Carmichael, Friendship: Interpreting Christian Love, London 2004.

13 By saying this I do not imply that these gifts are intrinsically connected to a homosexual identity, although this could be possible. But another possibility should also be kept in view, namely that the experience of cultural exclusion can often produce particular strengths in terms of sympathy and sensitivity.

such an identity good creational gifts and disturbances by sin have grown together. At the same time, this identity can be renewed to blossom in new ways under the calling of Christ. We should therefore find a path to do justice to the homosexual identity as it exists since the fall, both in this creational dimension and with this soteriological potential.

An individualistic culture like ours, in which personal relationships, as I have indicated, are burdened with high expectations, easily causes such homosexual friendship to intermingle with the erotic. Acts and feelings that were meant to be expressions of friendship come to bear connotations of the domain of sexual intercourse. Precisely here, do I look for compromise. It is possible that people really intend to develop their homosexual identity into forms of friendship and therefore to abstain from sexual intercourse. Yet, they cannot endure the individualistic form celibacy often is forced to take in the Western world. If that is the case, I am inclined to accept a form of friendship that intends not to be of an erotic character but yet in our culture cannot avoid some mixed feelings in which sexual undertones are not completely absent. By insisting on a complete purity of feelings in such a relation, we would almost rule out the possibility of genuine friendship between homosexuals in our culture.

This, thirdly, urges traditional theory to strive for more radical renewal. What we need is an alternative biblically inspired interpretative framework to understand homosexual identity and preference. Otherwise we would ignore the remaining differences between biblical and present day contexts and leave Christian homosexuals with the view that their homosexuality, in biblical terms, counts as a telling example of estrangement from God. They only would have an incomprehensible Divine Command, without a possibility to recognize their homosexuality as meaningful from the perspective of the gospel. We need a convincing narrative that helps them understand their homosexuality and the implied calling to celibacy not in the first place as a suffocating burden but rather as challenging gospel.

Richard Hays offers the first chapter of such a story. He points to the cross, new creation, and community as three focal images that direct the Christian life. This story should be lived, not only told. Its performers are to be found in the Christian community as such, not only among homosexuals. This narrative implies a new concept of kinship consisting of the life we share in Christ. This could balance our individualism and unite the married and singles within the one eschatological family. It could also transform our quest for authentic self-fulfilment and our sexual needs. Living this story requires an overall renewal in spirituality and life style.[14]

Exactly that awareness leads to the second chapter of an alternative story that perhaps could render present day Christian homosexuality as meaningful. Christian homosexuals summon the church to feel the necessity of this renewal. In the biblical context homosexuality counted as typical feature of a pre-Christian world without God. This was not meant to be a moralistic judgment but a motivation to seek this world with the gospel of Christ's love. In a certain parallel we could interpret the massive resurgence of the homosexual phenomenon since modernity as typical for the post-Christian world without God. But now Christians do not enter this world from outside; they always have been part of it and therefore participate in its features themselves. From a position within they must develop a counter-narrative and live a different life. Our post-Christian world too needs the gospel of Christ's love.

Could it be possible that this special position and calling are reflected in the phenomenon of Christians sharing in the homosexual predisposition and feeling themselves the attractiveness of the generally accepted lifestyle of today? Christian homosexuals then would be a kind of pioneers in living the biblical story in a post-Christian world. On the one hand they would typify the Christian solidarity from within. They witness the liberating grace and power of the gospel, even for our world. On the other hand their difficulties in upholding an alternative life of friendship in an individualistic and sexually liberal society remind the whole church of the urgency of their own renewal. This is not only indispensable in order to support their homosexual fellow-Christians but also would be the only way to fulfil its calling in this post-Christian context.

Sometimes, discussions between traditional and modern positions demonstrate tiresome replays of well-known old moves. With this effort to improve upon the existing traditional theory, I invite others to discuss it and do something alike with their approach. Perhaps this will open a renewed conversation.

14 Hays, Moral Vision, 193-205.

Homosexuality and Family as an Urgent Item for Church and Theology

Rinse H. Reeling Brouwer

1

During the early nineteen-sixties, Dutch pastors such as A. Klamer and A. J. R. Brussaard initiated a new approach to the church's attitude towards homosexuality. Klamer and Brussaard had experienced that homosexuals were not persons that were only encountered in rather exclusive ballet companies or exotic shows, but that they could be members of one's church parish, hiding their feelings, often leading a double life, being silent or having desperate conflicts with their spouses, being infinitely conscious of there anxiety and loneliness: young people who were doubting their future, honourable family men, and even preachers. These pastors organized self-help groups in which homosexual men and women could exchange their hopes and fears with one another. Some of these groups still exist today. The pastors tried to reflect on what they encountered in interdisciplinary groups with psychiatrists and others. They also tried to advance a public debate in church and society on their findings. Shortly thereafter homosexuals themselves ›came out‹ – in the spate of uprisings around the year 1968, this sometimes happened in the rather radical way of people struggling for liberation.

Today, half a century after this movement begun, after the establishment of many synodal study groups, reports and exhausting decision-making processes, the acceptance of homosexual men and women churches seems to have been increased in protestant churches[1]. Approximately sixty known homosexual ministers pastor congergations of Dutch protestant churches. Blessing (not consecrating) same-sex partnerships is now possible using the Protestant Church of the Netherlands' (PKN) special liturgy in the *Christian Service Book* (2004). Even in the more orthodox reformed and evangelical wings of our churches, the repudiation of homosexuality is not always and everywhere as massive as it was for some decades.

I will start off this short paper with the condemnation of homosexual behaviour, which, though not using such terms, Abraham Kuyper[2] pronounced in the chapter on Family in *Common Grace* (2). I will also evaluate his judgement of ancient Greek and biblical culture in the light of contemporary hermeneutic insights (3). I will then pass on to the consequences of the location of the question of homosexuality. I will consider those consequences for Kuyper, who treats homosexuality as in issue in family theology, which he views as an ordination of creation. I will also deal in full with the consequences for the similar location of their own experiences by many gay theologians (4). I will close this paper by developing some thoughts on (5) the relation of Christology and procreation and (6) that of Christology and identity politics for both sides of the argument.

2

According to Kuyper, the ordinances of State and Church only became necessary after the Fall. They are therefore in a certain sense of a more secondary character, whereas Matrimony was ordained in Paradise. By this logic, Matrimony has the genuine shape of an original ordinance of *Creation* and is genuinely independent of both State and Church (Kuyper 1904, 291ff.).[3] After the Fall, Sin tries to subvert this ordinance, by

1 Roman Catholic developments are a different story, chiefly on the side of hierarchy.

2 A. Kuyper, De Gemeene Gratie III. Het practische gedeelte, Amsterdam-Pretoria 1904.

3 The verse quoted in support is Gen. 2:24. Kuyper neglects de fact, that the movement which is described here is just the opposite of the practice of giving in marriage which takes place elsewhere in the book of Genesis (Chapters 24, 29-31 etc.) and therewith he neglects to ask for the reasons of this reversal.

means of passions, prostitution, adultery, rape and so on. ›It is enough to mention the name of the »secret disease« to see through this abomination.‹ ›The Holy Apostle has sketched us in Rom 1:18–21, in a very compelling way, how, by *this* exact passion, pagan life in the flourishing and mighty Roman Empire had eventually been undermined.‹ (o.c., p. 294). Even the excellent thinker Plato promoted such a tendency indirectly, by pleading for an education by the State, i.e. a failure to estimate the relation between a divine ordination before and after the Fall (o.c., p. 295). That had to do with the custom of the ancient Greeks, that estimated monogamy indeed, but only as a side issue, because with them the cult of the beauty of the body prevailed, ›and the proper desire of the Greek went out to free love, without any bounds or rule, let alone the abomination, of which Paul made mention in Romans 1, when the idolatry, that was committed with the beautiful body, did forget the difference between the sexes in the end‹ (o.c., p. 331).

Strikingly Kuyper omits carefully to mention the ›abomination‹, ›disease‹ or ›idolatry‹ of Romans 1 by name. The same is true for his emotional 1902 speech in Dutch parliament. He has observed terrible and horrible things ›schrikkelijke en gruwbare dingen‹). ›The evil at which I aim – I am not able to discuss the question publicly here – is the sin, for which God once turned cities into a valley of salt.‹ Napolean's Code Penal had, as a fruit of the French Revolution, cancelled the prohibition of fornication with a person of the same sex. In 1911, Kuyper, in coalition with the Roman Catholic politician Regout, would again take up an article (art. 248–bis) in the penal code that differentiated homosexual and heterosexual punishment for sexual intercourse with under age persons at the expense of homosexuals. This inequality was not abolished before 1971, so that the *Antithesis* between a Christian Puritanism and a ›heathen‹ tolerance – an ideological antithesis which was frequently constructed from both sides – would dominate a good deal of the 20th Century in the Netherlands.

3

What can we say about Kuypers views on ancient Greek customs in the light of more recent insights? In his criticism of Plato, he presupposes a difference between the domain of the *oikos* and that of the *polis.* This presupposition is correct in that Matrimony belongs to the domain of the *oikos*, which a woman is not required to leave, whereas erotic male-

male relationships are social functions in the domain of the *polis*. Michel Foucault[4] proved how difficult the situation was for a young male pupil in Socrates' school: to be loved by his master (as the passive partner) was an honour and an asset to his career. However, if such a relationship were to continue for too long, he would become known as an effeminate man, a thing unhelpful for one attempting to become a distinguished person in the general assembly (Foucault 1984, egg. 205–248). Kuyper's assertion that those customs exercised by a certain elite undermined political power is improbable, as later antiquity shows both a consciousness of the inherent problems outlined above, and a tendency to strengthen matrimonial structures, a tendency well matched with Christianity.

In the struggle against Hellenistic cultural domination, and in particular in the second century B.C.E., many Jewish movements might have felt the need to distinguish themselves from the Greek customs, especially on the field of decency (Zuurmond[5]). This could be articulated by aversions against nudity and same sex relationships. It might have been that context in which the ›homosexual‹ interpretation of the story of Sodom came up. This interpretation is not coercive to the exegesis of Gen 19:5, especially as canonical Scripture sometimes deems the violation of the right of hospitality the main sin of the city (Ezek 16:49; Matt 10:14.15). Under this interpretation however, the Gen 19 could support a resistance movement against an oppressive global culture (Jub 16:5f; Test Levi 14:6 etc), and sodomy becomes part of rabbinic lists of the sins of the heathen, of which Romans 1 may be one of the first still extant.

Abstracting such historical cultural struggles to an ›essence of homosexuality‹ across the centuries does not make much sense. I would not say (as G. Th. Rothuizen, and also the EKD do) that ›we do know more than Paul did‹. It is true that we know in another way, and that we know other things. The idea that a human is the owner of a sexual identity originates from the (western) Enlightenment, as does the concept of sexuality itself. Transferring those concepts to other cultures or times without further reflection is less than trivial. Traditionally, sodomy (which, byt the way, is a very broad concept), referred to an *act* that had to be punished, not to an inclination from which one has to be cured (as the old psychiatric schools thought) or, the other way around,

4 M. Foucault, Histoire de la sexualité 2. L'usage des plaisirs, Parijs 1984

5 R. Zuurmond, ›De zonde van Sodom‹, Wending 37(1982)5, 359-364

that has to be part of a process of self-acceptance (which is the more modern view). To this date, there are cultures in which friendships between two persons of the same sex with some corporal component belong to a certain normality, without being brought under the control of strong definitions and without undermining the value of matrimony for the same persons. David and Jonathan are an example, as are many North African cultures. For people embedded in western society, it is very difficult to think in terms other than those of our own (homo)sexual identities. This is one of the reasons I am very distrustful towards programmes that ›heal‹ that identity. However, on the other side, it is also true that representatives of western culture in global – and also in ecumenical – encounters often show a terrible lack of awareness of the ways of socialisation and the customs of other cultures and are inclined to impose their own ›struggle for gay rights‹ and so on upon others in a rather undifferentiated and unemphatic way. Without a hermeneutical conscience of the relationship of Biblical Witness and the multitude of cultures, our theological discussion will stagnate for a long time on this issue, too.

4

The theory of the Family as an Order of Creation by Abraham Kuyper is not free from the danger of omitting some forms of hermeneutical reflection. Moreover, it could unintentionally suggest that *some* cultural forms should be outside the realm of sin and inside a paradisical world, while in reality they are only *one* way of shaping sex/gender-relationships. One can understand the systematic and the strategic reasons to protect this domain from the grip of the State and the Church on it. Nevertheless, from the methodological point of view, it is hard to see how the processes of judgement and of liberation can be valued in this field when it is placed outside the reign of Redemption.[6]

66 Because of confessional objections against the doctrine of the Church of Rome, Kuyper refuses to subject Matrimony to the logic of Salvation. Reading the New Testament, it is questionable whether this view can be maintained. Cf. Hemelsoet (B. Hemelsoet, Marcus: verklaring van een bijbelgedeelte, Kampen 1977), who proved that Jesus in Mark 10:1-10 starts to speak on the relation of the Messiah and his bride (Jerusalem) and only afterwards, in the light of that, speaks on family relationships in the way of parables and likeness.

However, the same has to be said on the reasoning of some advocates of an acceptance of homosexuality in church and society nowadays. In our country, many people know the famous *dictum* of the late father Jan van Kilsdonk s.j., who helped many gay people with his (chiefly epistolary) pastorship: ›Homosexuality is a surprising invention (›een vondst‹) of the Creator‹. It connects with the feeling of gay men and women themselves: ›For God, I may exist as I am.‹ In no way I want to object these sentences as such; on the contrary, I accept the first one as a good sentence in preaching (›Predigtsatz‹), and the second one as a good sentence of faith (›Glaubenssatz‹). But for theological reasoning it is insufficient. It may strengthen the tendency, already present in the gay movement, to exhibit and to celebrate the own existence, or the own way of existing, as a good in itself and with that to blockade all self-critical questioning and all dialogue with others. Then one absolutizes one's own identity and forgets that this too merely is a certain historical form, a form in some way proper to be a parable of the Kingdom of Heavens, but at the same time, as all historical forms, subject to divine judgement and in need of divine justification.

In this way, one may also outcry oneself and the homosexual condition as such, neglecting the shady side of this mode of existence. Of course, human imperfection is not present in a certain part of the human race only, since human perfection does not exist in this world at this time. But we cannot deny that there exists a specific homosexual experience with human imperfection that has to be realized by the people who undergo this experience. There is the loneliness – every boy or girl has to discover for him- or herself that he or she ›be‹ gay –, the lack of predefined social forms, and for many, be it through divorce or through living outside the traditional domestic circle, exclusion from procreation, even though people in our culture have found inventive solutions to this problem. There are homosexual fathers that have a child with a woman, but raise it with their own partner, and there are homosexual women that ask a friend for a donation of sperm to have a child. Many things changed in the way of thinking about the forms of living together, of parenting and of being a family. However, these new forms cannot push aside the awareness of the tragic, or at least the negative aspect of creation (with its twofold character of day *and* night, dry land *and* water), and thus also of the life of a creature in its erotic disposition.

5

But this is not all that has to be said. Notwithstanding Kuyper, we have also to speak of kinship in the order of redemption. In classic thomistic thought, the *telos* of the sexual difference (including genital shape) in the human race is procreation, and the *telos* of matrimony is posterity (Nachkommenschaft). The sacramental grace of the Church thereupon presupposes and elevates this teleology. But is it possible to maintain these theses in a messianic reading of the Scriptures? Certainly: ›male and female He created them‹ (Gen 1:27). But then follows ›the Book of the generations of Adam, man‹ (Gen 5:1). And in all these *toledoth*, generations (›Zeugungen‹) of all human people that fill the earth, the literary telos in this book is the appearance of the firstborn son of *Israel* in the midst of many brothers and sisters (Breukelman[7]). In the first canonical gospel then, the ›Book of generation‹ in Israel appears to have as its literary telos that son in the midst of the brothers and (rather piquant) sisters, ›who is called *Christ*‹ (Matt 1:1.16). So, all the generations, the kinship relations that are related in short genealogical notices or in circumstantial Biblical stories, have their centre in and aim at the generation of the Messiah that gives all those other generations both their sense *and* at the same time their henceforth no longer *redeeming* sense. For rabbinical Judaism, where surviving as such is necessary to redemption, this cannot be said, but for the *ekklesia* that confesses the *parousia* of the Messiah, procreation does not have any redemptive force any longer. Therefore, in Christ both the family as of old organised around a heterosexual kernel, as well as others forms of community life or living alone have their – relative! – sense (Cf. 1 Cor 7). Nowadays, many homosexual men and women do prefer a shaping of their lives in the likeness and imitation of the dominant figure of marriage, and desire the acknowledgement of this on behalf of both the state and the church. On my part, I prefer a way of availability for the messianic kingdom outside that form, including its mirror image, that of ›same-sex marriage‹.

7 Breukelman shows how the superscription *elè toledoth* structures the book of Genesis as a whole: Gen 2:4a, 5:1, [6:9, 10:1, 11:10,] 11:27, [25:12,] 25:19, [36:1, 36:9,] 37:2; F.H. Breukelman, Bijbelse Theologie I/2, Het eerstelingschap van Israël. De theologie van het boek Genesis, Kampen 1992.

Consequently, rebirth (baptism) should be given priority over birth and the *ekklesia* over kinship relations. That community has to be a trainingschool (Calvin), also in training companionship in the field of sexual diversity, learning mutual acceptance and distinguishing mutual vulnerability – which then may be advantageous in family life, too. In the Christian gay liberation movement, as in most emancipation movements, there is a predilection for Paul's sentence ›in Christ, there is neither male nor female‹ (Gal 3:28), mostly understood as a war cry for equal rights in gender relationships. Now it is certainly right that the Apostle put fixed images and a fixed behaviour in social relationships into perspective in a fundamental way. However, in doing that, I think he simultaneously prevents the identification of any liberation struggle with the newness of Christ Himself. If I may paraphrase: ›in Christ, there is neither gay nor straight‹, you also have to realize that your possible ›gay identity‹ is *broken* in Him. ›He that glorieth, let him glory in the Lord‹ (1 Cor 1:31; 2 Cor 10:18 King James Version). If there is such a thing as a messianic vocation, it is not the affirmation of already existing vocations, but the breaking of those. It is not the affirmation of rights, but their ›making void‹ (Rom 3:31); not the strengthening of given identities, but their interruption (Cf. Agamben[8]) – ›the time is short; it remaineth, that both they that have wives be as though they possessed not‹ (1 Cor 7:29): that is not only said to honest family men, but to their (perhaps ›gay‹) antipoles as well! However, exactly this fundamental relativizing of given identities in the perspective of the eschatological *Parousia* of the Messiah could be the best starting point for a real conversation between the agents of those identities, both in the congregation and in theology.[9]

8 G. Agamben, The Time that Remains: A Commentary on the Letter to the Romans, Stanford 2005

9 The theology of neocalvinism during the second half of the twentieth Century also shows the tendency to think about phenomena as family relations not only in terms of creation, but also in terms of eschatology. Cf. A. de Bruijne in G.G. de Kruijf, P. Schaafsma (red.), Meer dan een optelsom. Kanttekeningen bij de waarde van het gezin, Kampen 2008, 125.

Kinship in the Light of Contextual Pastoral Care

A Relational Ethical Perspective

Kees Bregman

1 Introduction

Practical theology recently discovered the family as a theme through the so-called ›contextual therapy‹ of the Hungarian-American psychiatrist Ivan Börzörményi Nagy (1920–2007, henceforward Nagy). In the Dutch field of pastoral care Nagy's school of thought was adopted by Hanneke Meulink-Korf and the late Aat van Rhijn. As the founders of a two-year course in contextual pastoral care, they trained hundreds of male and female pastors in the theory, methods and practices of this particular form of pastoral care. This course is still taught by Annette Melzer and Kees Bregman.

In this essay I will briefly introduce Nagy's view on family ties, healing powers in the family and the application of his views to pastoral care.

I will put this contextual approach alongside the biblical commandment to ›Honour your father and your mother‹ and show how it is relevant to the transfer of faith from parents to children.

Practical Theology

How can a secular theory of social casework be translated to pastoral care? That is the first question we have to deal with. In my view the secular and religious fields cannot be reduced or converted into one another. However, both disciplines gain new meaning when compared and contrasted. A good example is the parallellismus membrorum of Biblical poetry, where the second line is not merely a rewording of the first: a new meaning arises in the interaction between the two lines. Similarly, the confrontation with Nagy's thoughts provides a new perspective on the theory and practice of pastoral care.

›Context‹

The word ›context‹ here has nothing to do with ›contextual theology‹. The term comes from a theory of social casework. Nagy's concept of ›context‹ has a highly specific meaning: *context is the dynamic and ethical interconnectedness – past, present and future – that exists among people whose very being has significance for each other.*[1] (BGT 8) Nagy's system of concepts seems rather static, like that of a bookkeeper. However, it is important to realize that he had lively relational processes in mind. We have to understand his concepts in a dynamic way.

The first people *whose very being has significance for each other* are parents and children. In a wider sense this also holds for grandparents and grandchildren and brothers and sisters. Their relationship is established by an irrevocable fact: birth. Nagy thinks that the consequential nature of relationships is ontological, based on the very fact of being. Family relationships are strengthened by the fact that the members *are* connected to each other by birth, rather than by what they *do* for each other. The need many adopted children feel to discover their biological parents in their country of origin is a clear illustration of Nagy's observation.

1 Ivan Boszormenyi-Nagy and Barbara R. Krasner, ›Between Give and Take. A Clinical Guide to Contextual Therapy‹, New York 1986. (Referred to by BGT and page number)

Contextual Therapy

Starting off here, Nagy defines contextual therapy as the approach based on the empirical knowledge that a person's fair consideration of his or her relational obligations can result in personal freedom to participate in life's activities, satisfactions and enjoyment. (BGT 414) Due consideration, that is, acting upon a fair balance of give and take, is a major relational source. This relational source liberates from a false or inauthentic sense of obligation. Due consideration also liberates from wasteful interpersonal conflicts. The main goal of contextual therapy is to help people find inner freedom in order to act fairly and duly in their family relationships.

Nagy stresses the importance of an open relationship with the extended family for the well-being of the individual. What does this mean in light of ambivalent family realities? We all know the reverse of family life: the pain and suffering people can cause their next of kin. We do not have to dwell on such horrible situations as child abuse or negligence, nor on extortion of parents by an addicted adult child. In the sphere of pastoral care we often deal with the more delicate troubles of family life: tensions arising from different interests, different needs and different views on faith or the life of faith. Yet the intention is the same: to help someone find personal freedom, not by breaking with relatives, but by balancing due care.

Four dimensions

How is Nagy mapping out the world of the family? He distinguishes four or five dimensions in the realm of relational reality. The first dimension covers the *facts*: socio-historical events, gender, genetic issues, position between siblings, adoption, divorce or loss of parents at a young age, and so on. The second dimension covers *psychological issues:* feelings such as anger and aggression, personal development, basic trust, and the like. The third dimension is *systemic*; it includes ways of behaving, transactional patterns, triangulations, and so forth. The fourth dimension perceives relationships in light of ethics. This is the dimension of *relational ethics*. It includes questions on loyalties, the fairness of the balance of give and take between family members, merited trust, (destructive) entitlement and the phenomenon of parentification: when children feel the urge to care too much for their parents. Nagy uses the vocabulary of accounting to express what happens in the fourth dimension.

Finally the idea of a fifth *ontic* dimension is a late development in Nagy's thought, derived from the dimension of *relational ethics.* The *ontic* dimension is concerned with existential dependence on others in order to live an autonomous life.

Nagy developed a secular theory. He considered religion, faith, beliefs and their correlative practices, such as church attendance, as belonging to the second dimension, the dimension of individual psychology. This is a momentous observation, for it would mean that the relational ethical dimension is more fundamental than religious convictions.

Loyalty

According to Nagy, loyalty is the main concept with which the impact of family relationships can be described. Loyalty refers to the undisputed fact of familial ties. Grandparents, parents and children have vertical loyalties. These are asymmetrical: parents usually care more for their children than vice versa. Brothers and sisters, chosen partners and friends have horizontal loyalties. These relationships are called symmetrical, for they are on equal terms. In a wider sense, there is also loyalty in relationships within extended, adoptive, foster and step families. Loyalty also comes into play in the relationship between in-laws and children-in-law. Present-day composed families exhibit many variations, but there is always a twofold core. This core is an existential alliance, which is established, firstly by the very fact of someone's birth, secondly by the good care someone received. Consanguinity is not decisive. Who cares for the child and provides subsistence matters enormously. In short: kinship is not merely genetic, but also involves lasting care.

From his work as a therapist Nagy observes that these existential loyalties are a source of trust. They constitute a relational resource. Balancing loyalties allows people to secure or recover their ›right of existence‹. Nagy explores this phenomenon in the fourth dimension of relational ethics. His presupposition (mainly taken from Martin Buber) is that human existence is fundamentally ethical. It hinges on what is fair and appropriate, on what give and take is just. In terms of bookkeeping: in every family there is a *ledger* of give and take, of damage and trust, of deficits and merits. Every generation is in need of good *balance* in the way people do justice to one another. Being responsible, not indifferent, is what someone needs to gain freedom to live his or her own life.

The observation that loyalty is not a feeling of alliance or relationship, nor a moral duty is important. A child is not obliged to be loyal to his parents; he or she simply *is* loyal, perhaps in a hidden or apparently contrary way. Loyalty, according to Nagy, concerns *being* itself. Loyalty is an existential category.

The concept of *entitlement* raises the same issue. Entitlement is an existential justification of give and take. For example, a newborn is entitled to being taken care of. Children are also entitled to express their affection towards their parents. If someone is not allowed to ›live entitled‹, he becomes ›over-entitled‹. Too much entitlement generates destructive feelings and behaviour. Trouble arises when someone is not allowed to live according to his or her loyalties. For example, when parents are divorced, children often face *split loyalty*, as they cannot connect positively to one parent without losing the affection and approval of the other parent. The consequence is that the loyalty these children so deeply feel is disguised, turning into a so-called ›*hidden loyalty*‹. In the long run the child may become entitled to act destructively against himself or others, examples being children or partners. Nagy called this a *revolving slate*: recovering from damage by inflicting damage on an innocent.

Therapeutic attitude: multi-directed partiality

Nagy derives his concept of *multi-directed partiality* from this concept of loyalty. Multi-directed partiality is his main instruction on how to act therapeutically. This concept is key in contextual pastoral care, too. Multi-directed partiality means that the therapist or pastor keeps an eye on the interests and entitlements of each of the family members involved. He consecutively takes on the perspectives of each family member, even those who are not present or who have already passed away. He therefore uses circular questioning. Instead of asking ›What does your mother mean to you?‹ he would ask ›What do you think you mean to your mother?‹, or ›What would your father say if he was asked about the meaning of your relationship with your mother?‹ This indirect, circular way of asking questions sets the balance of give and take in motion. It elicits the so-called *ethical imagination*.

The concept of ethical imagination was added to Nagy's contextual theory by Barbara Krasner. She describes ethical imagination as follows:

the capacity to picture and test what is owed and what is deserved in a given context – with equitable regard for the self and for the other.[2] In conflicts family members often blame one another unfairly. Unfair blame arises when people exclude the viewpoint of the other person in order to reinforce their own viewpoint. Yet one cannot justify one's own hurt feelings without having to assume responsibility for corrective action. The therapeutic and pastoral approach hinges on encouraging someone to put himself in the position of the other and to imagine the ›good reasons‹ he has to act the way he does. This opens up opportunities for ›direct address‹, entering into a renewed and genuine dialogue.

The contextual approach reaches out to remaining parts of mutual trust and trustworthiness. Nagy focuses on the sources of trustworthiness in the family itself, extended over three or even more generations. All the give and take of generations is remembered by an unwritten ledger of balances. The task of the contextual therapist or pastor is to help someone read, carefully and patiently, those balances of give and take, which involve himself and his significant others. The method requires time and patience. It often needs a sort of delay, a *moratorium*. The underlying loyalties in the family, whether visible or invisible, are always at work.

Contextual pastoral care, a description

How can Nagy's approach shape a pastor's view and pastoral attitude? *Contextual pastoral care*, as defined by Hanneke Meulink and Aat van Rhijn, can be described as follows: *We believe that in the presence of God, man always joins hand in hand with others, whilst at the same time, hand joined in hand with others, man is in the presence of God.*[3] The wording is poetical: a parallellismus membrorum. The first line emphasises one's uniqueness, the second one's interconnectedness, and both emphasise the ›coram Deo‹: ›in God's presence‹. Man, God, fellow man – is a triad with a hidden core. Meulink and Van Rhijn have called the ›coram Deo‹ an ›unsuspected Third‹. The *coram Deo* may be an implicit, silent dimension, but it is essential for pastoral care: we

2 Barbara R. Krasner and Austin J. Joyce, Truth, Trust and Relationships. Healing interventions in Contextual Therapy, New York 1995, p. 219.

3 Hanneke Meulink-Korf en Aat van Rhijn, De onvermoede derde. Inleiding in het contextueel pastoraat, Zoetermeer 2002, p. 51. (Hungarian translation: A harmadik - akivel nem szamoltak / Hanneke Meulink-Korf, Aat van Rhijn. - Cluj-Napoca 2009)

examine the ethical involvements of our relationships as we stand in God's sight. In other words: man is irrevocably responsible for others, while in his alliance with others he is standing on the firm ground of God's trustworthiness.

An example

Some considerations regarding the transfer of faith from parents to children will be presented as an example of the contextual approach. These days this matter is often raised within our church communities. The transmission of beliefs is frequently accompanied by a conflict of loyalties. This conflict of loyalties can divide grandparents, parents and children in a desperate way. Such conflicts are surrounded by feelings of guilt and failure before God. How do we deal with these ethical and religious involvements in contextual pastoral care?[4]

The first consideration is that children are entitled to be brought up ›well enough‹. Does this necessarily include some form of religious education or a certain orientation on matters of life? Nagy asserts this is mainly a desire of parents. He places religious convictions in the second dimension, that of individual psychology. The drive to raise children in faith would exist mainly to suit the fulfilment of parental expectations. As an ongoing and possibly hidden loyalty it reflects the inner drive of parents to act on the loyalty towards their own parents, obeying the family code: ›we are believers‹.

The contextual concept, which deals with this subject, is *›legacy‹*. Legacy is a transgenerational mandate. Legacy links the inherited endowments, the received gifts, of the current generation with its obligations to its own posterity. *Legacy is the ethical imperative for the present generation to sort out what is beneficial in life for the next generation's quality of life. Each person owes the future consideration of both the mandates and the missions of posterity.* (BGT 418). We are heirs of the future. Legacy is a positive, helpful notion. It contrasts with *delegation*. Delegation refers to negative transgenerational expectations. Examples are parental possessiveness or destructive behaviour like alcoholism. Whether good or bad, children themselves have to deal with their legacies and delegations. They have to weigh and sift all they

4 Contextuele Berichten, 10/3 Autumn 2005 on ›Geloofsoverdracht‹ (Transmission of Faith)

received from their parents and sort out what is vital to them. Every new generation is a new chance. Nobody is doomed to repeat the failures of his ancestors.

This view sheds light on the fifth commandment, ›Honour your father and your mother‹. Now what is ›honour‹? In Christian tradition this ›honouring‹ is often taken to mean ›obeying‹. It is an instruction to continue and copy the beliefs and Christian conduct of parents, never to change the church's rites and manners, to continue speaking the same language of faith. We all feel that this is impossible. However, parents hope their children will believe in God like they do, and parents feel guilty when their grown up children fail to do so. In the light of contextual thinking we find a remarkable aspect of the word ›honour‹. It literally means ›to give weight‹. This meaning can be paraphrased as follows: »Children, give weight to the burden your parents have taken by choice or by fate (this is *ethical imagination*). Give credit, acknowledge their love and trustworthiness (this is the *ethical perspective*) shown through their efforts to give you the best you need in life. Then, evaluate the ›weights‹ of your own efforts and find your own balance. Give your own mature answer.«

What is the value of transferring faith in such a way? It is valuable because the time and the world in which children live differ from those of their parents and grandparents. A new generation has to translate the old resources. Contextual theory learns us that the deeper bond is the loyalty that becomes visible in the actual process of the child sorting out what is useful and helpful to it. Faith presupposes alliance, but sincere alliance cannot exist without the right to be different. Every new generation is entitled to stand in its own unique authenticity before the face of the Holy One.

Index of Authors

Prof. dr. Henk van den Belt is Assistant Professor of Reformed Theology, Utrecht University, Faculty of Humanities, Department of Theology, on behalf of the Reformed League in the Protestant Church in the Netherlands.

Dr. Kees Bregman is a pastor of the Protestant Church in the Netherlands. He has acquired a doctorate in the field of homiletics. He practices as an independent contextual pastor and coach and is involved with the Foundation of Contextual Pastoral Care in the Netherlands.

Prof. dr. Ad de Bruijne is Professor of Christian Ethics and Spirituality at the Theological University of the Gereformeerde Kerken (vrijgemaakt) in Kampen.

Prof. dr. Zsolt Gereb is Professor of New Testament at the Protestantisch-Theologisches Institut Cluj/Klausenburg.

Prof. dr. Gerard den Hertog is Professor of Systematic Theology at the Theological University of the Christelijke Gereformeerde Kerken in Apeldoorn.

Dr. Elöd Hodossy-Takács is Associate Professor of Biblical Theology at the Debrecen Reformed Theological University in Debrecen.

Dr. Maarten Kater is Assistant Professor of Systematic Theology at the Theological University of the Christelijke Gereformeerde Kerken in Apeldoorn.

Andrea Pethö-Udvardi is PhD-student at the Evangelisch-Lutherische Theologische Fakultät in Budapest.

Prof. dr. Rinse Reeling Brouwer is Professor on the Miskotte / Breukelman Chair for Theological Hermeneutics, Senior Assistent Professor History of Christian Doctrine and Director of Education at the Protestant Theological University in Amsterdam.

Dr. Jan Roskovec is Assistant Lecturer of New Testament at the Protestant Theological Faculty of Charles University in Prague.

Dr. Petruschka Schaafsma is Assistent Professor of Ethics at the Protestant Theological University in Amsterdam.